AF610049

From a photographic print by Batchelder & Co, 1867:
Pictures Collection, State Library of Victoria, H29563

The Curate of the Wannon

A biography of the
Reverend Francis Thomas Cusack Russell
1823 - 1876

Alex. E. H. Stone

PO Box 118 , Milang SA 5256, Australia

ISBN: 978-1-4457-7173-1

Foreword

In 1965 I was appointed as the Anglican Rector of Coleraine and became aware of how much the church there owed to the pioneering work of the "Curate of the Wannon". There was even a large portrait of him hanging over the mantle-piece in the Rectory living room to remind me of his place in the history of the parish. This inspired me to try and find out more about this remarkable man.

Luckily the parish records included many documents relating to Francis Russell's ministry and through the kindness of the Winter-Cooke family I was able to supplement this information by reference to letters and other documents in the library at "Murndal", their historic home. I was also fortunate that one of the librarians who visited the branch library in Coleraine obtained copies for me of the publications which set out the events which describe Francis Russell's relationship with Bishop Broughton in Sydney.

The greater part of this account of the ministry of Francis Russell was written before I left the Parish in 1969 and was presented to the Coleraine Historical Society and subsequently printed in the Coleraine *Albion* over a number of issues. Since then the typewritten manuscript has been revised and augmented, transferred to several different computer platforms and programs and now forty years later is at last being made available to a wider audience in the hope that those who read it will share my admiration for the character and achievements of a truly remarkable Christian gentleman.

Alex. E. H. Stone

Chapter One

On Wednesday 19th November 1834 Edward Henty arrived in Portland Bay on the schooner Thistle with 13 heifers, four working bullocks and a few other animals, as well as materials for building a house and five companions. In this way began the first permanent settlement in the future State of Victoria. During the following months the Hentys continued to extend and build up their new establishment. They brought more stock over from Van Diemen's land, including the first merino sheep to arrive in Victoria, but their activities remained confined to the country round about Portland Bay.

It was not long, however, before they were to turn their thoughts and activities to new pastures to the north. This was brought about by the surprising arrival at Portland Bay, in August 1836, of Major Thomas Mitchell, Surveyor-General of New South Wales, who had travelled down the River Darling to its junction with the Murray and then been drawn to continue through Western Victoria, passed the Grampians and down the Glenelg River to the coast. Major Mitchell had been most impressed by the country through which he had travelled, calling it *"Australia Felix"* and he gave a glowing account of it to the Henty brothers Edward and Francis.

The result of this news of wonderful country to the north was an extension of the Henty's Pastoral activities to the rich valleys of the Glenelg and the Wannon and the eventual establishment of stations known as Merino Downs , Muntham, and Sandford. Of course the news of the opening up of such good grazing land could not be kept secret, and before long other squatters were settling in the Wannon-Glenelg area. Samuel Pratt Winter and his brother Trevor crossed from V.D.L. in 1837 and settled at Murndal and Tahara Bridge. Another early settler was John Robertson at Wando Vale.

As these settlers became established, others followed and settled down in various ways. Inns sprang up along the rough road from Portland to the Stations to the North. There were regular stopping places at what are now

Heywood and Digby, and other towns grew up at Casterton and Coleraine. The inns in these places were the venues for many local activities, including some of the first church services. The first Anglican services in the Wannon area were conducted by the Rev'd J. Yelverton Wilson of Portland but by 1850 there was a resident clergyman in the district with the spiritual charge of "Wannon cum Glenelg".

The Rev'd Francis Thomas Cusack Russell did not live in any of the towns in the district but had his parsonage more centrally located on a hundred acre block fronting the River Wannon close to the Coleraine-Merino road. The Wannon district has a very characteristic landscape of flat-topped ridges divided by the many valleys of the rivers and other streams. Francis Russell's Parsonage was built where one of these ridges slopes down to the river, just as the ground begins to level out.

Looking out towards the Wannon with its many meanders he would see the big old Red Gums which mark its course, but closer to the house he had planted a garden of fruit and other trees so that, like most of the early homes, the parsonage was surrounded by an oasis of deciduous trees which presented a marked contrast to the grey sameness of the native gums.

It is Tuesday 1st April 1851 and we move inside the house because of the arrival of a wedding party. The bridegroom is a shoemaker and his bride a widow. The couple stand before the parson while the latter reads the familiar words: "Dearly beloved, we are gathered together here in the sight of God, and in the face of this congregation, to join together this Man and this Woman in holy Matrimony..."

Then he addresses the man, "William, Wilt thou have this Woman to thy wedded wife, to live together after God's ordinance in the holy estate of Matrimony? Wilt thou love her, comfort her, honour, and keep her in sickness and in health; and, forsaking all other, keep thee only unto her, so long as ye both shall live?" And William answers, "I will."

The bride is similarly addressed, "Mary Ann, Wilt thou have this Man to thy wedded husband, to live together after God's ordinance in the holy estate of Matrimony? Wilt thou obey him, and serve him, love, honour, and keep him in sickness and in health; and, forsaking all other, keep thee only unto him, so long as ye both shall live?" And she answers, "I will."

The service continues and finally the newly-weds are blessed: "Almighty God, who at the beginning did create our first parents, Adam and Eve, and did sanctify and join them together in marriage, Pour upon you the riches of his grace, sanctify and bless you, that ye may please him both in body and soul, and live together in holy love unto your lives' end. Amen."

No doubt there was some light refreshment offered the happy party before they made their departure. It would also be noted that the parson did not expect any fee for his services. Ten years later it was mentioned in the *"Hamilton Spectator"* in a report from Coleraine that "the rev. Doctor is greatly esteemed here, indeed quite a favourite with all classes; and I am informed that the nice young girls of Coleraine, money or no money, can 'marry the boys', through the instrumentality and liberality of the kind-hearted, amiable, and talented vicar..."

At the time of the wedding that has been described, Francis Russell had been Curate of the Wannon for less than a year. Still less than thirty years old, he had already come into conflict with Bishop Broughton in Sydney and had been suspended from officiating by him. However in the years to come he was to earn the undying love and respect of the people of the Wannon District and held in high esteem by his clerical colleagues as well as by Bishop Perry the first Bishop of Melbourne.

Francis Thomas Cusack Russell was born in Dublin, probably in 1823 and grew up "by Killarney's lakes and fells". His father, the Reverend Thomas Russell was Vicar of Kilbonane, Kilcredan and Molahiffe near Killarney in County Kerry. In 1870 he wrote to a friend who had just visited that part of Kerry, "your feet pressed the ground I trod on in my go-cart, for Molahiffe and Castle Island and Kilbonane Parishes the union my father held, went to the brink of the lakes and embraced Mucross Abbey."

Thomas Russell was born in Kilkenny, the son of Francis Thomas Russell. He entered Trinity College Dublin in 1810 when he was seventeen and graduated B.A. in 1816. He was ordained Priest on the 25 April 1818 and took up his appointment in the united parish of Kilbonane.

He had married Bridget Anne Cusack in 1817 and they had three children Margaret, William and Francis. Thomas Russell died in 1823, the year in which Francis was born, when he was just thirty years old. By 1825 Bridget was living in Dorset Street, Dublin so Francis' reminiscences about Killarney may owe something to the imagination.

While Francis was still quite young he was taken care of by his mother's cousin, Sir William Cusack-Smith, *Bart.*. Sir William was a distinguished lawyer. He was Solicitor-General of Ireland from 1800 to 1801 and then succeeded his father as one of the Barons of the Court of Exchequer in Ireland. Young Francis was a particular favourite of his uncle and used to go with him to court and even sit beside him on the bench.

THE CHAPEL AT TRINITY COLLEGE, DUBLIN

Francis Russell's brother, Thomas William Cusack Russell, after attending Mr Turpin's School entered Trinity College Dublin in 1837. He graduated B.A. in 1846 and was ordained priest in 1849. In the seventies he was Curate of Hugglescote near Ashby-de-la-Zouch in Leicestershire and it was there that Bridget died on the 2nd February 1869 in her eightieth year.

When his uncle died in 1836, Francis Russell, now aged 13, was sent to the school at Middleton conducted by Mr Turpin. It was here that a life-long friendship began between Francis Russell and Peter Teulon Beamish who was later to become Archdeacon of Warrnambool. Peter Beamish has testified that at school his friend was of a notably serious disposition and became a leader amongst his school-fellows.

Francis entered Trinity College Dublin as a pensioner on 14 October 1842. For two sessions he attended the dissecting rooms and was considering a medical career, then he was thinking of studying law. He finally decided that he was being called by God to the Sacred Ministry and this determined the course of his studies. He had the B.A. degree and Testimonium in Divinity conferred on him in 1846.

While still an undergraduate Francis had read in the report of the Society for the Propagation of the Gospel extracts from a letter of the Reverend A. C. Thompson, the second Anglican minister to reside in the settlement of Port Phillip, outlining spiritual conditions there. This prompted him to offer himself to the S.P.G. for service in foreign parts and he also persuaded two of his college friends to do likewise. Early in 1847 the three friends visited Dr. Hinds, the secretary in Ireland for the S.P.G., in order to decide upon the fields of their future labours.

The result of this visit was that Francis Russell and Peter Beamish decided to go to Australia and William Russell (no relation to Francis) decided that he would go to China. William Russell does not come again into our story, but he was successful in learning to speak and write Chinese and in 1872 became the first Bishop of North China with his Cathedral at Ningpo.

Francis Russell was next examined by the Chaplains of the Bishop of London and would have been made Deacon if he had not been persuaded to wait until he had arrived in Australia. He was persuaded to do this because Bishop Broughton "complained that his office seemed to be slighted in that men from the home Universities, applying for work in his diocese, received ordination from the Bishop of London." However Francis did feel that there might be disadvantages in receiving colonial orders but he was assured that there would be none.

Before leaving for Australia, Francis Russell married Margarette, daughter of John Smithson of Bridge Street Dublin, a member of a Quaker family. (One of her cousins also became a churchman, and was later treasurer of the Diocese of Cork.)

ST AUDOEN'S CHURCH, CORN MARKET, DUBLIN

The wedding was celebrated on the 16th or 17th February 1847 at St Audoen's Church, Corn Market, Dublin. It is said that she was only thirteen when they were engaged and sixteen when they were married.

The Russells set sail for Sydney in the middle of 1847, together with Mrs Russell's sister Lucy, and Francis Russell's staunch friend Peter Beamish.

Chapter Two

Francis Russell arrived in Sydney, together with his wife and friends, in August 1847. In spite of the assurances of S.P.G. he was faced almost immediately with the question of the disadvantages of a colonial ordination. Bishop Broughton indicated that he required those whom he ordained to promise to remain in the country for ten years.

This unexpected requirement was probably the consequence of the terms of the Letters Patent by which the Bishop had received his appointment as Bishop of Australia. He was given authority to ordain a qualified person "especially for the purpose of taking upon himself the cure of souls or officiating in any spiritual capacity within the limits of the said Diocese of Australia and residing therein." These limitations to his ministry were to be distinctly stated in the Letters of Orders of any man ordained by the Bishop.

Francis Russell felt unable to make the undertaking required by the Bishop and the latter in the end did not press the matter. However, when he was ordained the Letters of Orders plainly stated that his ministry was limited to Australia. On Sunday 19th September 1847 Francis Russell and Peter Beamish were made Deacons in Saint Andrew's Cathedral Church. This was eventually to be replaced by the present imposing building, but a contemporary writer describes it as being "neatly erected of timber, and furnished in the interior with a reading-desk, altar-rails, chancel seats and stalls, and open seats for the congregation—all of beautifully-carved cedar, which species of timber grows abundantly amid the colonial forests. At the western end, over the principal entrance, is a gallery occupied by the Sunday scholars, whose voices are accompanied by the notes of a small but good-toned organ."

After his ordination, Francis Russell was appointed as Minister in the Parish of Alexandria (later to be known as Darling Point) with its temporary Chapel dedicated to Saint Mark. His friend became the Incumbent of Singleton, but requested the Bishop to make the appointment only a temporary one. In 1848 Singleton would be a part of the new Diocese of Newcastle, and he did not wish to be separated from his friend in another Diocese.

In the late forties, Sydney was a thriving city. Joseph Fowles in his *Sydney in 1848* is concerned by text and engravings to refute the discreditable reports which some people had been giving of it. The population of the city was 38,358 in 1846. There were several Banks, a Library, Museum, Botanical Gardens, a number of Public and Parochial Schools as well as the Anglican College at Lyndhurst and the Roman Catholic Seminary at St Mary's.

"Having reached the centre of the town, let us pause for a moment and look around us. Few strangers, we imagine, could do so on their first arrival in the metropolis of New South Wales, without the most lively emotions of surprise. In place of a paltry town which many of them are led to expect, they find shops and warehouses which would do credit to an European capital, offering for their convenience every article of comfort and luxury; while, in every direction, are to be seen unequivocal indications of progress and improvement. The handsome equipages that dash past, the elegantly clad females, and the stylish groups of gentlemen, point out the seat of amusement and gaiety. The heavily laden wains—the crowds that sweep past, in every direction—the hasty step of some, the thoughtful brow of others, betokening the purpose of intense occupation—all speak of extensive and untiring commercial activity."

Even Sydney's Penal Colony beginnings were beginning to fade. Transportation to New South Wales was abolished in 1840 and by 1847 Convicts formed only 3.2% of the total population of the colony. Also, since 1842, the colony's Legislative Council (composed of members appointed by the Governor and elected by the people) had been responsible for many of its affairs. At this time the Speaker of the Council was Dr. Charles Nicholson, a parishioner of St Mark's, Alexandria, who was to become the Colony's first Baronet. Many years later in a letter to Sir Charles, Francis Russell wrote: "Darling-Point was my first cure and the faces of the congregation of S. Mark's—yours in the foremost seat live in our memory."

At Alexandria, Francis Russell faithfully ministered to his parishioners, conducting the services of the Church in the temporary chapel. This was the only parish building and was used for the Sunday School which met prior to the morning service, and for the Parish School during the week. Naturally, as a Deacon, there were many of the Church's ministrations which he could not provide, but these deficiencies were made good by the Bishop himself who lived in nearby Darlinghurst. The latter commented that from the time of Francis Russell's ordination as Deacon "he had been resident near me; we had rarely passed a week without intercourse; and very few months in which I had not assisted him in the services of his Church, or in accompanying him to minister to the sick in his parish."

In 1848, in the normal course of events, he would have been ordained priest, but he was still concerned about the standing which would be enjoyed by a colonial clergyman who returned to England. The legal position had been eased late in 1847 when three new Dioceses in Australia were created and Bishop Broughton became Bishop of Sydney and Metropolitan of Australasia. The new Letters Patent made no reference to the subject of ordination and did not place any restrictions upon those ordained. The Bishop was therefore able to satisfy his doubts and he resolved to present himself at the ordination following.

The Bishop recalled that "he had made it a question whether ordination by a colonial bishop would entitle a clerk to hold a benefice in the United Kingdom; and the apprehension as to the degree in which this might mar his future prospects had occasioned Mr Russell to decline presenting himself for ordination at the expiration of the first year after his admission to the diaconate... I had shown him to his own satisfaction that his scruple was groundless, and had distinctly stated to him my own resolution, as one of the colonial bishops, never to lay my hands on another candidate for the office of the ministry, were I not persuaded that every one so ordained by me was fully competent to discharge all the offices of it in any Diocese of the Church, under the license of its proper bishop." To this the bishop received the following letter in reply.

Saturday, Rushcutters' Bay

MY LORD BISHOP,

I beg to return my sincere thanks for the kind and satisfactory reply I have received from your Lordship.

At the next Ordination after the approaching one I hope, D.V., to present myself for the office of Priest.

May I venture to remind your Lordship of your promise to officiate at St Mark's Chapel on Sunday next (to-morrow). I have given notice of the celebration of the Holy Communion.

I remain, my lord,

Your obedient Servant,

F. T. CUSACK RUSSELL

The Right Rev. Lord Bishop of Sydney

BISHOP WILLIAM GRANT BROUGHTON

From a lithograph by J.S. Prout based on a sketch by the Bishop of Tasmania. National Library of Australia an9454312

However not all of his associations with the Bishop were without incident. On Sexagesima Sunday, 11th February 1849 it was announced that on the following Sunday there would be the celebration of the Holy Communion, but the arrangement was altered at the Bishop's direction who then attended at Saint Mark's on the First Sunday in Lent, 25th February. When the Bishop arrived he was received by Francis Russell, but he could not enter the building immediately because of the Sunday School and had to wait a minute or two for the children to come out. The weather was not very favourable and this together with the sexton's child being dangerously ill caused a delay in the commencement of the service.

Later, during the celebration of the Holy Communion, by some mischance one of the women of the congregation was communicated with the Chalice before she had received the consecrated bread. This brought a sharp rebuke from the Bishop which was repeated in the Vestry after the service. Angrily the Bishop added, "Sir, many complaints have reached me as to the irregularities practised at St Mark's." Francis Russell replied that there was no truth in such accusations. The Bishop then instanced the omission of any morning service on Ash Wednesday. In reply it was mentioned that such a service would have meant the interruption of the day school and would have been attended by very few. Instead an evening service and lecture had been held and it was proposed to continue with this each week during Lent.

On the following Wednesday, 28th February, the Archdeacon of Cumberland, the Venerable William Cowper called on Francis Russell with a letter from the Bishop directing him to visit officially the Parish of St Mark, and charging the latter with "...evidently entertaining too slight a sense... of his obligation to submit himself to the injunctions of the Prayer Book, which he had bound himself by engagement in sight of the Church, that he would faithfully observe," Eight grounds were set out as a basis for this accusation. Most of them referred to matters which had occurred or been raised when the Bishop was visiting St Mark's on the previous Sunday.

The following day, Thursday 1st March, Francis Russell wrote to the Bishop replying in turn to each of the points raised. His letter then continued with an exposition of his own position as a Churchman contrasted with the activities of others whom he believed to be working against the best interests of the Church, that is those with Tractarian beliefs.

"I speak warmly because I write from a full heart; I yield to no man in love to the Church of England: none more ardently desires her prosperity; and it is just in proportion to this my desire I feel constrained to use all caution and circumspection. Our mission is to win souls to Christ; our Church, I believe, best fitted under the Holy Ghost to accomplish this, therefore do I try to enlarge her borders by conciliating her foes when honest, by unmasking them when dishonest, by abstaining from all hasty innovations, by a timely yielding of that which cannot be retained; by exercising a Christian charity towards the conscientious scruples of the weak; by infusing confidence in those distrustful of her regiment; but above all by a clear and full exposition of that precious Gospel from whence all her doctrines are drawn; which gives life to her decent forms, the beauty of holiness to her solemn services: and to her sacraments comfort and efficacy.

"Here, my Lord, you have a full exposition of my sentiments—my principles of action are before you. If you mistrust my discretion, I am, as I have often said, ready to carry out any general order you may publish, but do not seek to fasten upon me a charge of divergence from a rule notoriously by all set aside.

"In conclusion, I am sincerely glad if at last we are to enjoy the benefits of a wholesome and vigilant discipline; but do not, I entreat you, my Lord, give cause of triumph to persons who are in heart ill disposed towards you, who are ill affected to the Church, who have been betrayers of their trust, and false to their vows; mere pretenders to an enthusiasm they have never felt; entire bigots, and entire knaves; perverters of the gospel, and ruthless destroyers of immortal souls. Do not, I conjure you, the bidding of such caitiffs. 'Let not the sword of justice be at the assassins beck.'"

This letter, written in such strong terms because of the warmth of his feeling in the matter, was later withdrawn at the suggestion of the Archdeacon. And as the Bishop did not go on with his accusation the whole matter was allowed to lapse— for the time being.

Chapter Three

In the second quarter of the nineteenth century a call was made to the Church of England to realize its true nature as a part of the "One, Holy, Catholic and Apostolic Church". This call was embodied in ninety *Tracts of the Times* which were issued between 1833 and 1841 by the leaders of what we now know as the Oxford Movement. These "Tractarians" included such men as Keble, Pusey and Newman. Their teaching tended to emphasize the Catholicity of the Church with a consequential playing down of its Reformed nature.

To many Evangelicals this movement seemed to be merely thinly disguised Papalism, which was itself the work of the Devil. The subversive nature of the Tractarian Movement appeared to have been clearly shown when in 1845 the Rev'd John Henry Newman, its most notable leader and author of many of the Tracts, was received into the Roman Catholic Church, and was followed by a number of other members of the movement.

This position was duplicated in the young Australian church. A number of the local clergy had been influenced by the Tractarians, and even the Bishop was not unsympathetic. In a letter dated October 1837 he wrote: "You mention Mr. Newman's sermon. I have not seen it, for works of merit in that class come very rarely and slowly to these shores. But your introduction of his name reminds me to say that if I might make choice of my fellow-labourers, they should be from his school."

In 1850 Mrs Perry, the wife of the Bishop of Melbourne, was to write of him: "The Bishop of Sydney has an unconquerable aversion to a Presbuterian, and would, I believe, rather join hands with a Romanist. He does not seem to look with any alarm on the spread of Popery, and says that if all the priests were got rid of, the Romanists would all turn Protestants! and very likely they might; but how are the priests to be got rid of, I wonder?" Bishop Broughton was, however, strongly opposed to the claims of the Church of

Rome, and the S.P.G. in an address presented to him in 1853 commended him for "the steady resistance which you have offered to the encroachments and usurpations of the Church of Rome."

Francis Russell and Peter Beamish were both staunch evangelicals with a very low opinion of the teaching of the Tractarians. After coming to Sydney they became convinced that there was a Romanizing party within the diocese. Their worst fears seemed to be justified when the Rev'd R. K. Sconce who was Minister of Saint Andrew's, Sydney and a lecturer on the Thirty-nine Articles (a fundamental statement of Anglican doctrine) at the college at Lyndhurst became a member of the Roman Catholic Church, together with the Rev'd J. C. Makinson. This pessimistic view of the state of the Church in Sydney which was held by the two friends had an influence on the extraordinary events which occurred in the week ending 3rd June 1849 (Trinity Sunday).

It all began on Thursday 31st May. Francis Russell was travelling home from Sydney to Darling Point in an Omnibus with three parishioners. The conversation turned to a special collection which had been held the previous Sunday, Whitsunday, to support a fund for the increase of Colonial Bishops. He asked one of his companions, Mr Thomas Mort, what was the amount of the collections, and then commented that he was not sure that he "approved of the object for which they were made." He "did not think the increase of Colonial Bishops desirable, owing to there being no check to the power that they held."

In support of this opinion he quoted the case of Mr. Sconce, saying that the Bishop had been weak in allowing that gentleman to continue ministering at the Cathedral and teaching at Lyndhurst although it was known that he held Romanist opinions. Mr Mort spoke in support of the action of the Bishop on that occasion, to which Francis Russell replied, "I do not mean to say that the Bishop is at heart a Romanist."

From the Bishop, the conversation turned to the clergy in general. Again Francis Russell was critical of the actions of some of them. In fact he felt that "the state of the clergy in this colony was fearful, and that you could select better men from Norfolk Island" (The Penal Colony for the very worst offenders).

At last they left the omnibus and Francis Russell accompanied Thomas Mort as far as the latter's rooms. As they walked he spoke of a dispute which had arisen between Peter Beamish and the Bishop. He remarked that he considered the Bishop's conduct in this case to be "abominable".

Peter Beamish had been appointed to Singleton but did not remain there long after the arrival of the first Bishop of Newcastle. In February 1848 he became Deacon Assistant at St. Andrew's where the Bishop had temporarily taken charge until a new appointment could be made following the departure of the Rev'd R. K. Sconce. Then in April of the same year he was appointed to the district of Illawarra, including the centres of Dapto, Jamberoo and Kiama with Shoalhaven. It was uncertain that the District would be able to raise an adequate stipend so the Bishop undertook to provide £100 for the first year. However, when Peter Beamish had arrived in Australia he claimed that the S.P.G. had promised that he would receive £200 per annum with a parsonage. Because of this, in August 1848 when the Rev'd T. B. Naylor went to St Andrew's, the Bishop offered Peter Beamish the appointment to the now vacant Carcoar . This the latter declined, because of his concern for the people of Dapto and Shoalhaven. Then, at the end of April 1849 he received a note from the Bishop that the financial help which had been provided for the past twelve months would no longer be available.

There was no possibility of raising an adequate stipend locally, so Peter Beamish left Illawarra and returned to Sydney, applying to the Bishop for some other appointment. He replied that there was nothing available at present. The Bishop also enquired about arrangements at Illawarra for the safe-keeping of the Registers and for providing the ministrations of the Church in any cases of emergency. Peter Beamish's reply to this concluded: "As I conceive that I have been treated with great injustice, and as I know no cause for this, except it be my attachment to Protestant principles, I shall, if my claims are overlooked, hold myself at liberty to make our correspondence public, and to seek from the Colonial Legislature some determination of the matter."

The Bishop found this and a previous letter objectionable and the Archdeacon wrote at the request of the Bishop: "I must now, therefore, inform you that his Lordship, having those letters before him, cannot admit you to the order of Priesthood at the approaching Ordination; neither could I, conscientiously, present to his Lordship any Candidate so devoid, or so unmindful of the respect and civility due from a clergyman to his Diocesan." After this followed another letter, the language of which was so intemperate that, in spite of a later letter of apology, the Bishop would not consider ordaining Peter Beamish until September.

Shortly after Francis Russell parted from Thomas Mort, the latter had an interview on a legal matter with Mr Charles Lowe. In reply to a casual question, "What is the cause of Mr Russell being so violent against the Bishop?" Mr Lowe asked the reason for the question. Mr Mort then told him of the conversation in the omnibus and in the street.

The next day Mr Lowe wrote to the Rev'd T. B. Naylor, giving an account of what had been said during and after the journey in the omnibus and adding: "Now, my dear Sir, on hearing of these gratuitous and unguarded remarks proceeding from a member of the Church yet in his noviciate for her ministry; and upon the very day set apart for solemn humiliation and prayer preparatory to his ordination as a priest; [The Wednesday, Friday and Saturday between Whitsun and Trinity Sunday are Ember Days when prayer is made for the ministry of the Church and for those about to be ordained.] and comparing them, as I could not but do, with the solemn vows to which I heard myself the same member of the Church pledged as a Deacon, of reverent obedience to his ecclesiastical superiors, and knowing too from the notices given that he was about to offer himself a candidate for Priest's orders within two days, I did feel there was danger to the Church if such a step should take place with these things unrebuked; and being unable to divest myself of the conviction that not to declare them would be an act of infidelity on my part, I do with sorrow and shame report to you what I have heard.

"You are my immediate pastor, and I having thus unburdened my mind, I am content to leave the matter in your hands, pledging myself to substantiate this, if need be, though most unwilling to be brought forward as impugning a candidate for that ministry towards which, as a body, I feel so sincere a reverence."

It was also on the Friday that, as part of the preliminaries to his ordination which was set for the following Sunday, Francis Russell had an interview with the Bishop. This interview was described by the Bishop in a letter to the Archdeacon dated 5th June 1849. "...on Friday last, (the 1st instant,) we passed nearly three hours together; discussing amicably, and I trust, not unprofitably, subjects so sacred preparatory to his approaching ordination as might bestow upon that interview even a solemn character. In the course of it he acknowledged that both he and Mr Beamish had been in the habit of lending their ears to the insinuations and criminatory assertions which were perpetually made in their presence concerning me; and he very ingenuously said he was sensible they had done wrong, and regretted that he had been led by such inducements to believe almost anything to my prejudice. But Mr Russell added, 'it is impossible to help giving credit to what one hears perpetually repeated.' In the existence of such an impossibility I did not profess myself a believer.

"Nevertheless, perceiving how the case stood, that mischievous persons, no friends to the Church of England, had taken advantage of the inexperience and ductility of these young men, to impress them with such views as suited their own purpose, and had made them in fact their engines for discharging their malignity against myself. I allowed it to pass; and Mr Russell having expressed regret that he had yielded to such impressions, we separated in perfect charity and satisfaction (as I thought) at an advanced hour on Friday afternoon."

Chapter Four

The next day, Saturday 2nd June, Francis Russell attended at the Registrar's Office at 11.00 a.m. in order to complete the preliminaries to his ordination. In the presence of the Bishop he took the oaths of allegiance to the Queen and of canonical obedience to the Bishop of the Diocese, and made the other subscriptions required by the rules of the Church. Being very concerned that his friend had been excluded from ordination on this occasion, Francis Russell urgently desired the Bishop to grant an interview to Peter Beamish who had accompanied him to the Registry. Much to his distress this request was not granted. During his interview he had appeared excited or nervous and on leaving the Bishop the latter gained the impression "that Mr Russell quitted me with something very like menace as to the consequences which would follow from my determination."

This impression was confirmed by the Deputy Registrar, Mr H. K. James who wrote, in reply to a question from the Bishop: "When Mr Russell returned to the outer office where Mr Beamish was awaiting him, I continued to observe that he appeared very discomposed: and when he informed Mr Beamish that your Lordship declined seeing him, the latter remarked that 'then the case must be published,' or words to that effect. Mr Russell rejoined with some earnestness, that 'certainly all must be published,' or an expression of that sort, which led me to suppose that something further was intended. Mr Russell and Mr Beamish then took leave, and retired in evident displeasure."

As they were leaving, Francis Russell pressed his friend to make one more attempt to see the Bishop. So Peter Beamish sent in "by the messenger a polite message with my compliments for a moment's conversation on particular business with his Lordship." Francis Russell wrote later, "As the Bishop had, at this time, declared his intention of entrusting Mr Beamish with the cure of souls on the 15th June, confidently expected that his request, thus humbly put, would be acceded to. Shortly after, Mr Beamish overtook me, and communicated the painful answer which his Lordship had returned to him by the office messenger."

In the meantime, the Rev'd Beagly Naylor was concerned as to what action he should take as a result of receiving Mr Lowe's letter, especially as he was to be one of the three priests assisting at the ordination on Sunday. At last he decided to visit Francis Russell so that he could inform him of what he had heard in order that he might have an opportunity of contradicting it if it were untrue.

When Mr Naylor arrived at the house he found Peter Beamish and Francis Russell together so he asked for a few minutes private conversation with the latter. Mr Naylor then spoke of the rumour which had reached him concerning some comments which Mr Russell was reputed to have made about the Bishop. Mr Naylor later described the interview in this way: "I told him that in my present state of health, and about to leave the colony, nothing but a positive duty could have induced me to apply to him on such a subject, but that as the statements made to me affected his character, were injurious to the Bishop, and were made at a moment when I was about to be brought into so solemn a relation as regarded his ordination, I felt that I had no alternative but to take the course I had followed, and I prayed him to believe that I had only done that which under similar circumstances, I should wish to have been done to myself."

"He assured me that no apologies were necessary, and that he should have considered that any clergyman who had heard such a statement made about a brother clergyman, would have been forgetful of his duty if he had not acted as I had done. As to the statements themselves, he contradicted the portion which I had alone mentioned to him, and said that he had never uttered a word which could by any ingenuity have been distorted to such a purpose, and further, that he did not think anything of the kind."

Of this interview Francis Russell himself wrote, "The Rev. T. B. Naylor called on me on Saturday afternoon, and stated that a rumour had reached his ears to the effect that, in an omnibus, I had said with reference to the collections of Whit-Sunday, that 'they would be ill-applied in sending out to the Colonies POPISH BISHOPS LIKE DR. BROUGHTON.'"

After this matter had been concluded to Mr Naylor's satisfaction, the conversation turned to the Bishop's treatment of Peter Beamish and Mr Naylor gained the impression that some legal proceedings against the Bishop were contemplated on his behalf. This was later strongly denied by Francis Russell. The conversation did, however, take a legal turn because of the arrival of a Mr Dowling. Francis Russell said he felt great interest in the study of Constitutional Law, and that he purposed reading Halifax on Civil Law, and some of Justinian, with a view of proceeding to a degree in that science, if his life were spared.

Mr Naylor said that he thought it an interesting study, and Mr Dowling added that Civil Law was growing into more favour every day. Francis Russell asked whether there were any civilians among the colonial barristers, to which Mr Dowling replied that Mr Lowe was the only one. He also asked if reports were available of two matters concerning the Bishop, one with regard to an Ecclesiastical Court and the other an action against the Bishop. Mr Dowling also mentioned that he had obtained Burn's Ecclesiastical Law which Francis Russell had wished to consult on several points.

Some mention was also made of the way in which the students at Lyndhurst had been subjected to improper teaching because Mr Sconce had been allowed to continue lecturing on the XXXIX Articles even after his Romanistic tendencies were known. Mr Naylor protested that this was not true, but was not able to convince his hearer. When Mr Naylor left he was quite happy with the result of his visit. He said himself, "We parted with mutual expressions of good-will, and I felt thankful that a matter which seemed so full of perplexity had terminated satisfactorily."

After Mr Naylor had gone, Peter Beamish was told of the object of the visit. He asked if Francis Russell had not demanded the name of the person who had passed the calumny to Mr Naylor and was told that he had, and that Mr Naylor had answered him that it was a mere rumour.

During the latter part of the afternoon Francis Russell was away from home. He was concerned about obtaining the signatures of three clergymen on the letters testimonial which are normally required by candidates for ordination. He had not heard from the Rev'd W. Stack of Campbelltown to whom he had written, and although the Bishop had not asked for the document he was concerned about his position. It was for this reason that he particularly wished to refer to Burn's Dictionary. And for the same reason he went late on Saturday afternoon to St Leonard's to see the Rev'd W. B. Clarke—who unfortunately was absent from home.

When he returned home Francis Russell still had a number of matters to attend to. In spite of this his friend felt compelled "to point out to him that he had been compromised in his interview with Mr N., and that he would not be justified in allowing the insult to pass unnoticed". He "felt too that there was need for his acting with strict propriety, inasmuch as Mr Naylor was not likely to have undertaken this errand of his own accord, but was clearly acting at the instance of unfriendly parties."

This prompting from his friend led to the preparation of a letter to Mr Naylor which was to play an important part in the events in the Vestry of St. Andrew's Church the following morning, Trinity Sunday, 3rd June 1849. For an account of these events we can again draw on Mr Naylor's statement.

"At 11 o'clock, the usual hour of commencing Service, there were present in the Vestry, the Lord Bishop, the Archdeacon, the Rev. George King and myself, together with Rev. T. H. Wilkinson, candidate for Priest's Orders, Mr T. Druitt, candidate for Deacon's Orders, and Mr Robert Campbell, Churchwarden. The Bishop, notwithstanding the time for commencing Prayers had arrived, intimated his wish that we should wait a few minutes longer for Mr Russell. Shortly afterwards Mr Russell hastily entered the Vestry, and placed a letter in my hands, a duplicate of which he handed to the Bishop."

Saturday night, June 2nd, 1849
St. Mark's, Alexandria.
REV. AND DEAR SIR,

With reference to our conversation to-day, I wish you distinctly to understand that neither expressly nor by implication did I ever affirm that the Bishop of Sydney was a Popish Bishop.

Were it not for the low tone of morality which apparently prevails here I would have resented such a question, based upon mere report, as the grossest insult which could be offered. But I feel as if no clergyman of our communion had a right to be affronted by any suspicions or queries.

I can make every allowance for the enquiry you made, and indeed, I cannot think it an improper one when I call to mind (as you no doubt did) that a charge was publicly made against not a few of the Clergy of this Diocese, and that too by <u>name</u>, (which charge was never publicly denied;) —a charge so serious that were it not uncontradicted and avouched from a personal knowledge of the fact one could hardly give it credence, —I allude to the disclosures made by the Rev. R. K. Sconce, viz., that certain clergymen were accustomed to debate "whether the falsehoods the Bishop was in the habit of uttering were to be accounted as deliberate violations of, or carelessness about the truth."

This disgusting picture, degrades in a degree the whole body and denudes every clergyman of the privilege of feeling hurt by injurious suspicions or calumnious questions.

I remain,
Faithfully yours,
F. T. CUSACK RUSSELL

Continuing Mr Naylor's description of the scene— "While I was perusing it [the letter] I was interrupted by an expression of regret from the Bishop that there should be at such a moment any unkind feeling between Mr Russell and myself. I assured his Lordship at once that he was mistaken, that I had seen Mr Russell the previous day on a subject to which a portion of the letter referred, and that having parted from him on friendly terms, I was at a loss to contemplate his present proceedings. In an agitated manner Mr Russell addressed me, saying 'I have to ask you whether it is not Mr Walsh who is at the bottom of all this?' He was upon this checked by the Bishop, who deprecated the intrusion of such a subject at so solemn a moment, and said he trusted that we would give an evidence of the absence of unfriendly feelings. Upon this we instantly shook hands. His Lordship, who had not read the letter, then asked me whether I was willing to assist in the Ordination. I at once replied that I should be guilty of an act of hypocrisy and unfaithfulness to the Church, if, after what I had just read and seen, I should consent to be a party to Mr Russell's Ordination, and I handed the letter to the Archdeacon to read.

"Whilst the Archdeacon was reading it, the clergymen present were endeavouring to prevail upon Mr Russell to withdraw it, upon this I said that the mere withdrawal of the letter would not be sufficient, he must disavow the imputations it conveyed. The Bishop at this moment turning to me asked whether I would proceed with the ordination, to which I replied, 'No, my Lord, I feel that the letter of Mr Russell contains grave charges, and such as prove together with the whole of his present proceedings that I ought not to assist at his ordination.' His Lordship still appeared not to have read the whole of Mr Russell's letter, and therefore to be under the impression, that it was a matter personal to Mr Russell and myself, said to Mr Russell, 'This is most painful. Mr Naylor refuses to take part in your ordination, and under such circumstances I cannot proceed.' Mr Russell replied 'I am prepared for either case.' The Bishop then rose to leave the vestry.

"I felt shocked and distressed at Mr Russell's position, my own heart was heavy, and I conclude these feelings were expressed in my looks for as I passed Mr Russell, our hands were mutually extended and he said, 'I do not blame you in the matter Mr Naylor, I have no personal feelings against you.'"

Chapter Five

Letter from the Bishop of Sydney to Francis Russell.

Darlinghurst, 4th June, 1849

REVEREND SIR,

Trusting that the heat and excitement which you were labouring under yesterday have in some measure subsided, I address myself to you, as my duty requires, upon the very painful and unbecoming occurrences in the vestry of St. Andrew's.

I conceived at your first coming that your course of proceeding was really actuated by the complaint which you stated you had to offer against the Rev. T. B. Naylor. It excited my disapproval that under any circumstances you could have felt justified in reserving such a complaint till then, or in preferring it at such a time and place. The subject, as I understood, had been before you from the previous day. You were within a short distance of me; and know that you could at all times have access if you had any statement to offer; an access of which you had never hesitated to avail yourself at any season or hour of the day when objects of your own required it.

But on attentively reading your note to Mr Naylor afterwards, I was compelled to come to the conclusion that its being addressed to him was a mere blind; and that your real intention was to offer an insult to the bishop, from whom you were professedly seeking ordination; and to whom you had but the day before taken the oath of canonical obedience. Upon what ground such a course should have been pursued towards one to whom you stood in that relation, one who was so far your senior in years as to have been a minister of the Church long before you were born, and who had always conducted himself towards you with courtesy and candour, and I must add with extreme forbearance, your own conscience can best explain to you.

What I now have to say, is, that more years than I may probably have to live, will, to all appearance, be needed to restore you to that spirit in which you might becomingly present yourself again to me for ordination to the priesthood. After what has taken place my own confidence in you would scarcely be so re-established as to enable me with satisfaction to lay my hands upon you in that solemn rite; and therefore I must express myself unable to look forward to any such change of circumstances as could entitle you to ask (or me to grant to you) admission to the priesthood so long as I remain at the head of this Diocese. I wish this to be considered as my reply to your communication of yesterday, and that it may be final.

Whatever matters or arrangements there may be, connected with your parochial charge, other than can be transacted through my Secretary as heretofore, I shall be ready at all times to attend to, if proposed to me by any clergyman whom you may depute; but I cannot receive you again into my house; and must decline all correspondence in writing for the time to come.

With inexpressible sorrow, yet in perfect charity
I am, Reverend Sir.
Your very faithful servant,
W. G. SYDNEY.

The Bishop's hope that his letter would be the final word in this matter was not to be fulfilled. It could hardly have been delivered when, on the next day, Tuesday 5th June, two advertisements appeared in that morning's edition of the *Sydney Morning Herald*, one signed by Francis Russell, the other by Peter Beamish. Peter Beamish set out some of the events which had led to the Bishop refusing to ordain him (including some of the relevant correspondence) after writing this introduction— "The accompanying correspondence is of sufficient interest to a large number of your readers to entitle it to a place in your journal. For my own character's sake it is necessary that I should account for my exclusion from the order of Presbyters."

Francis Russell wrote— "To prevent false reports and evil surmises, I think it my duty to offer to those interested in the welfare of the Church of England a correct version of the extraordinary proceedings which took place previous to the late Ordination in St.Andrew's Church." He then went on to give an account of Mr Naylor's visit to him on the Saturday afternoon and of the events in St Andrew's Vestry, and made the following comments on Mr Naylor's action.

"Mr Naylor had a perfect right to refuse his assistance in my ordination; and was, no doubt, guided in his decision by a conscientious motive. I do not wish to prefer any complaints. My responsibilities are tremendous enough without the accession of the more solemn vows of the Priesthood. And the time which must elapse before I can become a Presbyter, if by God's grace improved, will make me the more experienced for its duties.

"It would be affectation in me to pretend ignorance of the current report, namely, that the 'question' was a scheme of the Romanizing clique to draw from me an intemperate reply, or a flat refusal to return any answer to such an insulting inquiry, with a view to debar me from the Priesthood.

"This was not I think and hope the case. In common with some of my brethren in the ministry I have rendered myself obnoxious to some of that unprincipled party and I heartily trust I shall ever be so; —for this is no struggle between high and low Church; —but the cause of God against the devices of Satan..."

The Bishop's reaction to these publications can best be gauged by reference to a letter written by him on the same day to the Archdeacon in which he also asked that a conference of the clergy and churchwardens be held in order to consider the whole of his dealings with the two Deacons.

Darlinghurst, 5th June, 1849

MR ARCHDEACON,

You have read, I am sure with feelings of shame and apprehension, which will be shared by every member of the Church, a publication in the *Sydney Herald* of this morning, bearing the signatures of the Rev. F. T. C. Russell and the Rev. P. T. Beamish. That an attack of this nature, which I cannot describe otherwise than as virulent, and which I know to be perfectly unfounded, should be made in this manner upon their Bishop, by two Deacons, almost the youngest among the clergymen in my Diocese, does occasion me feelings of shame and apprehension, which I again express my assurance that you will participate in. I cannot subject myself to the degradation of undertaking to reply to them through the same channel. At the same time I cannot be devoid of anxiety that yourself, and my brethren of the clergy, and the faithful members of the Church of England in general, should not be left wholly dependent on the very imperfect and inaccurate statements which have been made public under the abovementioned signatures.

My request is, therefore, that you will do me the favour to peruse the accompanying correspondence and documents, and that having done this, you will, if you deem it expedient, convene a meeting of the clergy of Sydney, and invite the attendance of one or more of the Churchwardens of each parish, and submit the papers to them. I do not wish to prescribe any particular course of proceeding, except requesting you to communicate to me what impression they make upon you, and upon the minds of others, lay and clerical, whom I have suggested you should associate with you...

The Bishop then proceeded to give some of his own observations on the two cases and also appended a number of letters and other documents, including a statement by Mr Naylor regarding his visit to Francis Russell and the subsequent events.

There was a meeting of the clergy and churchwardens as suggested by the Bishop, following which the Archdeacon conveyed their request to him that the whole of the correspondence should be published. The Bishop agreed to this, in a letter to the Archdeacon dated 14th June, and as a result the pamphlet entitled *Correspondence between the Right Reverend The Lord Bishop of Sydney and Metropolitan and the Reverends F. T. C. Russell and P. T. Beamish Deacons* was issued.

In a postscript to the pamphlet the Bishop wrote— "But for the concurrence of so many circumstances indicating a fixed premeditated design to avenge his own discontent with the Bishop and the whole body of the clergy, even at the expense of that faithfulness which he had sworn to maintain, the postponement of Mr Russell's ordination might have been regarded as the result only of certain personal differences which might be so obliterated by mutual explanation, as to leave no lasting blame attached to any party. But this exclusion from the office of the priesthood cannot now be regarded but as a note of the censure of the Church, inflicted for a very grievous and unprovoked violation of her holy discipline.

The Bishop, however, must have considered that some more positive action should be taken in the matter. On Monday 25th June he wrote to Archdeacon Cowper and the Rev'ds W. B. Clarke and J. C. Grylls, requesting them to act as a commission on his behalf in order to enquire further into the allegations made by Francis Russell and Peter Beamish.

Mr Russell was to be asked to give replies to the following questions:

A. What were his grounds for speaking of a 'Romanizing clique' (in his advertisement in the *Sydney Morning Herald* of 5th June 1849) which was 'an unprincipled party' engaged in a struggle which was not 'between high and low church, but between the cause of God against the devices of Satan'.

B. In the light of the last paragraph of Mr Russell's letter to the Bishop of 1st March 1849, would he name the persons to whom he refers and offer proof that they were '1. in heart ill-disposed towards me; 2. ill-affected to the Church; 3. betrayers of their trust; 4. false to their vows; 5. entire bigots and entire knaves; 6. perverters of the Gospel; 7. destroyers of immortal souls; 8. caitiffs and assassins.'

C. To give proof of the allegation contained in the following passage from a letter published in the *Sydney Morning Herald* on Saturday 23rd June. "My condemnation was of the teaching at St James' College, and the conduct of some who maintained the doctrine of the Church of Rome, whilst acting as ministers of the Church of England, and not of the clergy generally."

The Bishop had intended that Mr Beamish should also be required to produce proofs of allegations made by him, but finally decided against it because "...I am persuaded he is so incapable of curbing the fury of his temper, and measuring the effect of language, and has also exhibited so many proofs of disingenuousness in hazarding assertions which the slightest enquiry might have satisfied him were false, even if he did not know it at the time, that I should consider it only as investing him with a degree of importance to which he has no title, if any further consideration were bestowed upon his statements."

Francis Russell received a letter from Mr H. K. James, the Bishop's Secretary on 28th June, informing him "that his Lordship has addressed a communication to the Venerable the Archdeacon, with the Rev. W. B. Clarke, and the Rev. J. C. Grylls, constituting them a commission to receive from you such information and evidence as you may be desirous to afford upon certain matters, in connection with which, observations made public under your signature have recently attracted the attention of his Lordship." The nature of the points of enquiry was to be further explained by the Archdeacon himself.

Before this commission had begun its investigation an attempt was made to achieve a reconciliation between Francis Russell and the Bishop by two of the parishioners of the parish of St Mark's, Darling Point; Dr Charles Nicholson the Speaker of the Legislative Council, and one of the Church-wardens Mr Thomas Whistler Smith. On the morning of Tuesday 3rd July these two gentlemen waited upon the Bishop. They brought with them a letter from Francis Russell which had been addressed to them and which, after it had been read out by Dr. Nicholson, they were allowed to leave on the Bishop's table.

St. Mark's, Sydney, July 3, 1849

MY DEAR SIRS,

It has given me extreme pain that my note to the Rev. T. B. Naylor has been interpreted in a way utterly discordant with my real sentiments. I am sincerely sorry that I ever wrote so unguardedly, and I am now sensible that my letter may be capable of an ill-meaning, which, however, I earnestly declare I never intended it should bear.

Under these circumstances, with the exception of the first paragraph, which I would even more forcibly re-affirm, I now beg leave to withdraw the note, with an expression of my unqualified sorrow that I ever penned it. I further freely acknowledge the impropriety of presenting the letters above referred to on the morning of the Ordination.

I remain
Faithfully yours,
F. T. CUSACK RUSSELL

To the Hon. the Speaker of the Legislative Council; and Thomas Whistler Smith, Esq.

Mr Whistler Smith gives us this account of the conversation which then took place: "...his Lordship mentioned that he had been informed that Mr Russell had been engaged for three hours on the Saturday preceding the Ordination, in making searches for the report of an action brought against the Bishop by a clergyman some time ago. On our appearing surprised, the Bishop promised to obtain a statement in writing from his informant, saying 'it was but fair', that Mr Russell should have an opportunity of refutation.

"His Lordship also stated that the charge Mr Russell would have to answer was this, namely, his assertions as to the existence of a Romanizing clique, inasmuch as if such a party did exist it was necessary his Lordship should know it, in order that he might, as was his duty, take measures for the correction of the evil."

The following day, Wednesday 4th July, the Bishop wrote to Dr. Nicholson rejecting Francis Russell's letter as a sufficient apology. He also required that reparation should be made to the Rev'd W. H. Walsh for introducing that gentleman's name with an accusation which has been shown to be groundless. He again alluded to Mr Russell's occupation on the Saturday afternoon of Mr Naylor's visit and concluded by indicating that the results of the commission led by the Archdeacon would be an important factor in his final decision in the matter.

On Saturday 7th July the Bishop again wrote to Dr. Nicholson, enclosing a letter from the Rev'd T. B. Naylor the informant he had spoken of at their meeting on Tuesday. The Bishop's letter concludes— "Owing to the difficulty with which Mr Naylor is able to write, some delay has arisen in his furnishing me with the particulars called for. He has however at length supplied them; and I have the honour to forward them to you, that, if you should deem it expedient to communicate them to Mr Russell, an opportunity may be afforded him of seeing them before Mr Naylor leaves the colony, which will be, I believe, on Monday next."

Mr Naylor, in his letter, affirmed that Mr Russell had indicated that he was contemplating legal proceedings against the Bishop but made no mention of his searching for three hours for the report on an action against the Bishop.

The Bishop's letter, together with that of Mr Naylor, was forwarded to Francis Russell, but he did not receive them until Monday evening. Immediately he wrote to Dr Nicholson denying that he had contemplated any action against the Bishop. He commented that if Mr Naylor had gained the impression that that was his intention it was strange that he had affirmed in his Statement published in *Correspondence* that he left Mr Russell's house on the Saturday afternoon "thankful that a matter which seemed so full of perplexity had terminated satisfactorily".

Francis Russell added a postscript to his letter— "As Mr Naylor employed an amanuensis, may I express my regret that his letter, dated 4th of July, did not reach the Bishop until Saturday the 7th, at three o'clock in the afternoon, especially as Mr Naylor has sailed to-day for England, so that my contradiction could not be in time for his departure."

Chapter Six

In the meantime Francis Russell had received a letter from the Archdeacon concerning the commission appointed by the Bishop, of which he had had previous notice in a letter from the Bishop‘s Secretary Mr H. K. James. He was in some doubt about the purpose and authority of this commission and his reply seeking clarification of these points initiated a correspondence which lasted some days.

Sydney, 7th July, 1849

REV SIR,

The Lord Bishop of Sydney has requested me, in association with the Rev. J. C. Grylls, to receive from you such explanations, or statements, as you may be prepared to offer upon some expressions which appear in certain letters written or published by you, and reflecting upon the character of the clergy; in accordance with his Lordship‘s wishes we shall meet on Monday, the 9th July, at 11 o'clock A.M. at St. Philip‘s parsonage, and trust you will have the goodness to attend at the same time and place.

I remain, &c.,

WILLIAM COWPER

St. Mark‘s, Sydney, 9th July, 1849

DEAR MR. ARCHDEACON,

I have to acknowledge the receipt of your note dated the 7th *instant*, informing me that "you, together with the Rev. J. C. Grylls, have been appointed by the Bishop to receive from me such explanations as I may be prepared to offer of expressions published or written by me reflecting upon the clergy."

Before saying anything about myself, I beg to ask in what capacity you call upon me for explanations.

If you are sitting as a judicial tribunal, by what authority is that tribunal constituted, and of what specific offence is it to take cognizance?

If you are not sitting in a judicial capacity, but only as friendly referees to whom any statements I might wish to make are to be submitted, I apprehend that it is only reasonable that I should have been consulted in the selection of those in whom my confidence might be reposed.

Venerable Sir, with entire respect for your office and valuable personal qualities,

I remain, &c., &c.,

F. T. CUSACK RUSSELL

The Archdeacon's reply to this was also written on Monday the ninth and stated that the information was being requested for his Lordship's information and that the Bishop had "authority to inquire into the behaviour of any of his clergy". He also proposed a new meeting time, the following day at twelve o'clock. Francis Russell did not attend at St. Philip's parsonage nor reply to this until the Wednesday because his legal adviser was absent from town. He then wrote that his original queries had not yet been satisfactorily answered and concluded by raising another point. "...I am advised by counsel not to reply to any interrogations, the answers to which might lay me open to actions in the Supreme Court, which, although determined in my favour, would nevertheless be attended with considerable expense." To this the Archdeacon replied that the inquiries which he was directed to make were "entirely confidential, and cannot subject you to any actions in the Supreme Court." He concluded by renewing the proposed appointment at St. Philip's parsonage for the following day, Thursday the twelfth.

Francis Russell was still not satisfied and wrote to the Archdeacon on Thursday, "...I am still uninformed as to the objects, limits, and authority of that jurisdiction before which I am summoned to answer certain interrogations." He also felt that "it is most unusual authoritatively to demand from any person confidential communications" "Besides, I apprehend there would be a great injustice perpetrated were any person or persons to be compromised by statements which, under the seal of secrecy, they could have no opportunity of rebutting." The reply to this was merely a brief note signed by both the Archdeacon and the Revd J. C. Grylls with which was enclosed an extract from the Bishop of Sydney's Letters Patent (dated 25 June 1847).

"And we do by these presents further declare, that the aforesaid Bishop of Sydney, and his successors, may exercise full power and authority, by himself or themselves, or by the Archdeacon or Archdeacons, or the Vicar General, or other Officer or Officers hereinafter mentioned, to... call before him or them ...at such competent days, hours, and places, when and so often as to him shall seem meet and convenient, the aforesaid Rectors, Curates, Ministers, Chaplains, Priests, and Deacons, or any of them and to enquire as well concerning their morals, as their behaviour in their said offices and stations respectively..."

The next day the Archdeacon wrote again with a final ultimatum to Francis Russell from the Bishop which incidentally threw some light on the questions which had been raised.

Sydney, 13th July, 1849

REVEREND SIR,

Having transmitted to you an extract from the Bishop's Letters Patent, shewing by what authority you have been required to give explanations of the expressions in your letters before mentioned, I now beg to acquaint you with his Lordship's further instructions, conveyed to me in a letter dated 11th *instant*, but which I did not receive until after my return from Church last evening about nine o'clock. The Bishop says "I request that you will have the goodness to intimate to Mr Russell, that unless he, within five days from the present date (Sunday excepted), do put in a satisfactory reply to the questions which I have authorized you to propose, I must consider that he has no proofs to offer of the truth of the several assertions which he has circulated against the clergy, and shall proceed to express my sentence therefore as if the CHARGE against Mr Russell of circulating false and scandalous misrepresentations of the behaviour of the Clergy or some of them, had been admitted, or fully proved.

I desire also to have it known that there are privileged communications recognized by the law, and that among them are such communications as may be made by a Clerk in Holy Orders to his Bishop, when by such Bishop they shall be from him required, *bona fide* for the maintenance of due discipline; and if any undue use be made of such communications, the penalty in civil courts will fall upon the Bishop, who shall so use them contrary to law, and not upon the Clerk by whom they were, in honesty and in discharge of his duty, committed to the trust of his Ecclesiastical Superior." The inquiries which you are desired to answer, I enclose in order that you may be able to make the required statement within the time prescribed by his Lordship's letter.

I remain, Rev. Sir,

Your obedient servant,

WILLIAM COWPER

Rev. F T. C. Russell, St. Mark's.

QUERIES

In your letter published in the *Sydney Morning Herald*, 5th June, 1849, you spoke of a "Romanizing clique," and an "unprincipled party;" likewise of the "cause of God against the devices of Satan." Will you have the goodness to say who are the Persons to whom you refer, in the words "clique" and "party"; also, in what sense you use the expressions, "the cause of God," and "the devices of Satan?"

In your letter of 1st March, 1849, addressed to the Lord Bishop of Sydney, you alluded to some persons who are, "1. ill-disposed towards the Bishop; 2. ill-affected towards the Church; 3. betrayers of their trust; 4. false to their vows; 5. entire bigots and entire knaves; 6. perverters of the Gospel; 7. destroyers of immortal souls; 8. caitiffs and assassins." Will you. be so good as to state who are those persons?

In your letter published in the *Sydney Morning Herald*, 23rd June, 1849, you state that your "condemnation was of the teaching at St. James's College, and the conduct of some who maintained the doctrines of the Church of Rome, whilst acting as ministers of the Church Of England." Be so good as to state the particular teaching which you condemn, as also to name the Ministers to whom you herein refer.

WILLIAM COWPER

In the meantime Dr. Nicholson had continued his efforts to bring about a reconciliation between the Bishop and Francis Russell, whose letter of the

9th July he had left with the Bishop on the morning of Tuesday the tenth. The Bishop found the letter with its protest against Mr Naylor's allegations quite unacceptable. He wrote to Dr. Nicholson, "I can attach no weight whatever to so very flippant a production; and it compels me involuntarily to despond as to the probability of any such change being wrought in Mr Russell's temper and spirit as would enable me to regard him with those sentiments of respect and confidence which, for the general good of the Church, ought to prevail between us." The Bishop also showed the letter to the Rev'd T. B. Naylor who had not yet sailed for England. The latter denied "as plainly, as distinctly, and as solemnly as I can find words to do so, the whole of the assertions made in that letter." He asserted that following his conversation with Mr Russell on the second of June he was convinced that he "either for himself or another, contemplated an action at law against the Bishop of Sydney, to aid him in which he was seeking information."

There was still some question of the reliability of Mr Naylor's recollection of the events of the afternoon of Saturday, 2nd June. In speaking to the Bishop and also to Mr W. G. McCarthy he had asserted "that on the day preceding that of his expected ordination, after he had made his vows of canonical obedience, he was engaged three hours searching the records of the Supreme Court office, for the particulars of a case in which the Reverend Mr Brigstocke had sued the Bishop, and was making enquiry after the most skilful barristers and attorneys in civil law to assist him in certain proceedings which he contemplated against his Bishop." But in his various written statements he had made no mention of Mr Russell spending three hours searching the records of the Supreme Court. On Tuesday 10th July Mr McCarthy visited Mr Naylor at the particular request of Francis Russell. In response to a direct question on this point Mr Naylor dictated the following reply.

"If in my verbal report of what I have said in reference to my interview with Mr Russell on the 2nd June I am supposed to have said that Mr Russell was engaged (as above) I have been entirely misunderstood— I never said so: nor was there anything during my interview which could have led to such a supposition. I adhere minutely to my written statement, every word of which I solemnly declare to be true."

Dr Nicholson raised this point with the Bishop but the latter felt that it was not necessary "to enter into a conflict of disagreeing memories between Mr

Naylor and Mr Russell... because, if no more be taken than is admitted by the latter, as to what occurred at their interview, I think it perfectly sufficient." This was in a letter dated 12th July in which the Bishop also regretted that Dr. Nicholson's friendly efforts as a mediator had not met with success. The Bishop had already written to the Archdeacon (on the eleventh) instructing him that Mr Russell was to have five days in which to justify some remarks contained in his published letters. The Archdeacon's letter reached Francis Russell on Saturday 14th July and the latter's reply, dated 18th July (Wednesday) was sent to the Bishop by the Archdeacon and Mr Grylls with this covering letter.

Sydney, 19th July, 1849

MY LORD,

In conformity with your Lordship's letter of 25th *ultimo*, directing us to inquire into the several charges preferred by the Rev. F. T. C. Russell against a party which he alleges exists in this Diocese, we have placed before that gentleman the several questions suggested by your Lordship, and have this day received from him the Paper herewith transmitted, sealed when presented to us, and we have authenticated the same by our signatures, but of the contents of the document we are entirely ignorant,

We have the honour to be,

Your Lordship's most obedient Servants

WILLIAM COWPER

J.C. GRYLLS

Chapter Seven

Francis Russell's reply is dated July 18th, 1849 at St. Marks', Sydney, and begins by acknowledging receipt of the Archdeacon's letter containing the queries to which the Bishop required answers. He then makes a protest against the form of the present proceedings. "I must here say, that calling upon me to prove certain facts under pain of condemnation, before a tribunal precluded from receiving testimony upon oath, or compelling the attendance of witnesses does not seem accordant to any principle of equity." He also points out that the Bishop has made an assumption when he presumes that Francis Russell was referring to the "clergy or some of them" when he spoke of a "party" in the Church.

Finally, before proceeding to reply to the queries he asserts that his hesitation to reply to the Archdeacon's interrogation was not the result of wilful disobedience to the lawful authority of the Bishop but came from a desire to know what was the object of the inquiries. He indicates that this concern was justified because although the Archdeacon had assured him that it was "for the Bishop's information" it had now been asserted that "a failure of proof of certain allegations would be deemed and dealt with as an offence proven against me."

In reply to the first query about his use of the expressions "Romanizing clique" and "unprincipled party" Francis Russell writes at length concerning his view of the Tractarian movement in the Church, which he condemns for its abandonment of the true principles of Protestantism and its adoption of "Romanism or Romish doctrines". In support of his view he quotes from the writings of a large number of bishops and other church leaders. So far he has written in general terms, now he refers specifically to the local situation.

"25. I arrived in Sydney in July, 1847, and found it very generally believed that such opinions as I have enumerated were held in private, and even openly maintained, by a party in the Diocese.

“26. Certain overt acts were pointed to as betraying their intentions and identifying the ‘movement’ here with that in England.

“27. Amongst other things, it was known that a person in Holy Orders, and having cure of souls, received from the Incumbent of a Sydney parish, in the presence of two other clergymen, all of this Diocese, the form of ‘anabaptism’ an act of solemn mockery I believe unparalleled in the annals of our Church.

“28. I found, too, that a pamphlet had been extensively circulated, and even sold in the Depository of the Diocesan Society, intituled ‘Reasons why I submit to the teaching of the Church,’ containing Tractarian (even Romish) opinions, in their most matured form, edited by a gentleman whilst in Deacon’s orders, afterwards ordained Presbyter, and appointed minister of the Cathedral Church.

“29. I also learned that this gentleman had been selected to occupy the important function of Lecturer on the Articles of the Church of England in St. James’s College, and (as I afterwards heard), that during his ministrations he took occasion to state that in his opinion the decrees of the Council of Trent, on the doctrines of original sin and justification by faith, (that is, anathematizing all who profess the fundamental doctrines of Protestantism,) were the evangelical and proper statements.

“30. I found too, newspapers (the *Southern Queen*, and at a subsequent period the *Australian*,) under a management which displayed the easily recognized features of the Tractarian school.

“31. Suddenly all my worst suspicions were confirmed; two of “that party” (long associated together not only in friendship but in doctrine and purpose) at length convinced of the incompatibility of their opinions with the formularies of the English Church, passed from our pulpits to the service of the Church of Rome.”

Francis Russell then goes on to express his conviction that there was still a party within the Diocese holding Tractarian ideas. Amongst the indications which he cited in support of this was the fact that after Mr Sconce had left St Andrew’s, at a meeting of parishioners “a gentleman who is generally supposed to exercise no slight influence in the Diocese, was rebuked by the Chairman for attempting to deliver a panegyric upon Mr Sconce, in the presence of those whose spiritual interests he had betrayed.”

He also felt that the management of the *Sydney Guardian*, a church paper, was in the hands of men with Tractarian ideas who had used the paper to make an attack upon him. For this reason he was most concerned that the Revd J. C. Grylls who was officially associated with the *Guardian* had been appointed by the Bishop to form, with the Archdeacon, the Commission of enquiry. "...in a most indecorous manner they [the Tractarian party] have employed that journal to vent their virulence against me, and by so doing have placed the respectable clergyman whose name and character they have used to mask their proceedings in a most painful position before the public. Associated with yourself, Venerable Sir, in the Commission issued to try me, it is revolting to every feeling of justice, that he should seem to be connected with the publication of an article where my words are dishonestly quoted, my motives and character most foully misrepresented, and a sweeping and unjust condemnation pronounced against me."

In connection with the question of the *Sydney Guardian*, Francis Russell had enquired of Mr Grylls about the management of the paper—apparently through the kind offices of the Rev'd W. Stack. As a result the following memorandum was recorded on 12th July 1849 and later forwarded to the Bishop.

"The Rev. F. T. Cusack Russell having requested from the Rev. J. C. Grylls , (who is associated with the Venerable Archdeacon Cowper, by the Lord Bishop of Sydney in a commission to receive from Mr Russell explanations of expressions, alleged as reflecting upon the clergy, or some of them), the names of his co-editors, or the committee of management of a paper intituled *Sydney Guardian*, in which appeared an article complained of by Mr Russell as injurious to him, Mr Grylls declined acceding to Mr Russell's request." This was signed by the Archdeacon and Mr Grylls in the presence of Mr Stack.

The Bishop's second question was concerned with some expressions in a letter written by Francis Russell to the Bishop on 1st March 1849 in reply to some accusations which the Bishop had made about his conduct of affairs at St.Mark's, Alexandria. He had written of persons who were "ill-disposed towards the Bishop" and "ill-affected towards the Church" in rather strong terms. He felt that in answering the first question he had already sufficiently justified his words. However he does make one or two comments about the use of these words in a charge against him.

"44. I may remark, that as this letter [in which the expressions appeared] was withdrawn by me at your instance, I cannot think it otherwise than hard that the expressions used in it should be reproduced against me.

"45. A letter, be it remembered, written in answer to an accusation of the gravest character, brought against me, upon grounds all admitting of easy explanation or refutation, at which I felt deeply hurt: had I not felt so, I would have shown a carelessness about the opinion of my Bishop which I would hope never to experience. Neither can I admit that expressions contained in a letter to the Bishop can form part of a charge "of circulating false and scandalous rumours," &c.

"46. I may add, that his Lordship, after this letter had been three months before him, expressed his perfect willingness to admit me to the order of Presbyter."

In the third question he was asked to give details of the teaching at St James' College, Lyndhurst which he had condemned in a letter to the *Sydney Morning Herald* on 23rd June 1849 and to which he had referred when he spoke of "some who maintained the doctrines of the Church of Rome, whilst acting as ministers of the Church of England." His reply is as follows:

"47. The teaching at St James's College I condemned because Romish opinions were inculcated by Mr Sconce.

"48. Recent disclosures exhibit the dangerous effects upon a candid mind of such teaching.

"49. The conduct of any clergyman who maintained the doctrines of the Church of Rome, whilst acting as minister of the Church of England, I could not but condemn, were my moral sense not altogether blunted."

We have now almost come to the end of Francis Russell's long reply to the questions put to him by the Bishop through the Archdeacon. Our *resumé* of it can be fittingly concluded in his own words.

"50. In conclusion, I would beg to observe, that the charge now preferred against me of circulating false and scandalous accusations reflecting upon the clergy or some of them (there is, as I have before said an assumption here, as "party" was the expression I used), presupposes some moral offence; and I think, from the above statement, it will appear that I uttered but the strong and deliberate convictions of my own mind, formed upon a review of the events which I have detailed, and of many others which it is needless to particularise (as I cannot compel testimony), that there does exist in the diocese a party holding Tractarian opinions, which tenets the most exalted prelates have repeatedly denounced.

"51. Of course I offer this statement in self-justification, not by way of accusation against others, as I am the respondent, and not the promovant.

"52. Indeed to demand from me proofs other than I have given, would be to dismiss every recognized principle of justice, and cannot of course be contemplated; as no power is given to me of summoning or compelling the testimony of witnesses.

"53. I would only add that others beside me have drawn like inferences from the same facts, and I believe from careful observation of the opinions of the laity, that these facts have been deeply considered, and have exercised a powerful influence upon the minds of all earnest men; moreover, that if a distinct line be not drawn between 'Tractarianism' and the true principles of the Church of England, the worst consequences may be expected to befall our communion in this diocese.

"54. This conviction it was, that extorted from me the language for which I am now called in question."

The official reaction to Francis Russell's reply was the following communication from the Archdeacon.

Sydney, 23rd July 1849

REVEREND SIR,

I beg leave to inform you that the Lord Bishop of Sydney purposes on Wednesday next, the 25th *instant*, at ten o'clock in the forenoon, in St. James's Vestry, to express his decision upon these matters which his Lordship has recently had under consideration, namely— First, the occurrence in the Vestry of St. Andrew's on Sunday, the 3rd June, 1849. Second, the question then proposed by you, *viz*: "Be candid, Mr Naylor, is not Mr Walsh at the bottom of all this?" and Third, the public assertion made by you as to a Romanizing party, and the teaching at Lyndhurst. Upon the latter point the Bishop has received the statement in explanation forwarded by you, and his Lordship will form his determination upon the contents of the same. On the other two points he conceives that from personal observation he is competent to decide.

I am also to acquaint you, that if you have any concession to make or explanation to offer upon these first two points, his Lordship will be prepared to hear them in the Vestry room at St James's on Wednesday, before he pronounces his decision.

I remain, Reverend Sir,

Your obedient servant,

WILLIAM COWPER

Chapter Eight

On Wednesday morning, then, Francis Russell attended what was in fact an episcopal court in the Vestry of Saint James' Church. It could be said that this was a most appropriate venue for such a proceeding. The church building, one of the notable surviving examples of the work of Francis Greenway, was originally planned as a Court-house, and work begun. However, in 1819 the Government Commissioner Mr J. T. Bigge ordered that the building should be changed into a place of worship instead of proceeding with the erection of Saint Andrew's Cathedral, for which foundations had already been laid.

Those present in the vestry included the following clergymen: Robert Allwood (St James'), W. H. Walsh (Christ Church, St Laurence), George King (St. Andrew's), Francis Cameron (Balmain). Seven parishioners from Saint Mark's, including the Parishioners' Churchwarden, Thos. Whistler Smith, concerned about their pastor were also present. And also there, at the request of the Bishop, were the Bishop of Newcastle, the Right Reverend William Tyrell, and Archdeacon Cowper.

For an account of the proceedings we have two sources of information, one from either side. On the one hand is a pamphlet entitled *Report of the Proceedings in the case of the Rev'd F. T. Cusack Russell*; comprising the preliminary observations and the sentence passed; by the Lord Bishop of Sydney, Metropolitan, with an appendix of documents; and on the other a pamphlet containing a statement by Francis Russell and copies of many of the relevant documents furnished by him as the result of a request from his parishioners.

At ten o'clock the Bishop entered the room and took his seat. When the Bishop was settled, Francis Russell rose and approached him, asking "My Lord Bishop, am I to be heard now?" to which the Bishop replied, "Certainly not now, Mr Russell." He then began to read a prepared statement concerning the charges against Francis Russell preliminary to pronouncing judgement in the matter.

"Few persons who reverence the Church of England and desire that its welfare and stability should be preserved, can turn their thoughts to the circumstances of the case on which I have now to pronounce a decision without experiencing much uneasiness. None who give me credit for those feelings which, as the chief minister of that Church, I ought to entertain, but must be convinced of the extreme sorrow which these proceedings have occasioned me. The complaints which I have had to make of the conduct of a clergyman placed under my jurisdiction, that is the Rev. Francis Thomas Cusack Russell, the licensed minister of St. Mark's Chapel, in the parish of Alexandria, are to be ranged under the following heads..."

While the Bishop was reading, Francis Russell interrupted him, saying, "I have the Archdeacon's letter; am I not to be heard?" "No, Mr Russell" was the reply. "What are the charges? Am I not to know the charges?" To this the Bishop replied, "They will be stated immediately," and went on reading.

"First that he, on Trinity Sunday, in the present year, when attending at the Church of St. Andrew for the purpose of being received into the Holy Order of Priesthood, did contumaciously, in the presence of the Archdeacon and other clergymen, deliver to me, the bishop and ordinary of the diocese, and to the Rev Thomas B. Naylor, one of the clergymen attending me on the business of the Ordination, letters written by him (the Rev. F. T. C. Russell) of an insulting nature, and intended to insult, and also tending to incite strife and offence, contrary to his engagement and duty as a Deacon, especially on such an occasion and in such a place.

"Secondly, that he (the Reverend F. T. C. Russell). addressing the Rev. T. B. Naylor, used these words "Be candid. Mr Naylor; is not Mr Walsh at the bottom of all this?" or words of like effect; thereby calumniously attributing to Mr Walsh (that is the Rev. W. H. Walsh, licensed minister of Christ Church) and to the Rev. T. B. Naylor, a confederacy in some design to the detriment of the Rev. F. T. C. Russell, of which he had no proof to offer, and of which they were not guilty.

"Thirdly, that in certain printed statements, under the signature of the Rev. F. T. C. Russell, and published by him in the *Sydney Morning Herald*, it is insinuated that "a Romanizing clique" and an "unprincipled party", in this Diocese had acted with a view to debar Mr Russell from the priesthood; and it is declared that he condemned the teaching of St. James's College; and the conduct of some who maintained the doctrines of the Church of Rome whilst acting as ministers of the Church of England; which accusations he has not confirmed by any evidence, although duly required, and having had sufficient opportunity afforded him to produce such evidence."

Again, while the Bishop was reading Francis Russell exclaimed loudly, "Two of the charges I never heard before." and "That charge is false." He became so excited and upset that some of those sitting with him were moved to restrain his movements and the Bishop called upon him to be silent, under the obedience that he had sworn to him. There were differing interpretations of Francis Russell's efforts to have the opportunity to speak. Later on the same day the Bishop wrote a memo which included this comment. "These interruptions, sufficiently disrespectful in themselves, were rendered still more so by the tone and manner which accompanied them: a tone of studious provocation, and a manner peculiarly contentious and offensive such as showed evidently that in claiming to be heard he was bent only upon offering me every kind of insult."

A similar interpretation appeared in an article published in the *Sydney Guardian* on 1st August 1849. "We shall not attempt a description of Mr Russell's deportment in the Court. It was so exceedingly insulting that it was impossible for his Lordship to allow him, at that time, to be heard, as we understand had been contemplated." This comment so aroused Mr Thos. Whistler Smith, Churchwarden at St. Mark's, who had been present in the Vestry at Saint James', that he placed an advertisement in the *Sydney Morning Herald* of the 3rd August. After referring to the article in the *Guardian* he then set out the Archdeacon's letter to Francis Russell and followed it with an attestation signed by all the laymen from St Mark's who had been present unofficially at the proceedings in the Vestry.

"With relation to the above communication we attest that we were present in the Vestry room of St. James's, Sydney, when the Rev. F. T. C. Russell attended... and that before the Lord Bishop commenced to read his judgement, the Rev. F. T. C. Russell attempted respectfully to address his Lordship in allusion to the said letter, and that during the time of the delivery of the sentence, appeals were made by the Rev. Mr. Russell to be heard, but his Lordship peremptorily refused to hear him, and insisted, in fulfilment of his oath of allegiance, upon his keeping silence under pain of deprivation of orders."

WM. DUMARESQ

JOHN STREET

J. C McLAREN

EDWARD KNOX

GEORGE J. ROGERS

THOS. WHISTLER SMITH

EUSTACE SMITH

The Bishop continued to read his prepared statement which reviewed the events in the Vestry at St Andrew's on the day of the Ordination and those which had taken place on the day before, particularly Mr Naylor's visit to Francis Russell. With respect to the first charge against him, the Bishop concluded: "...I cannot entertain a doubt, that in presenting himself professedly to receive ordination, Mr Russell came with a studied purpose to offer me an insult, and to provoke, if possible, strife and discord between myself and the clergy. Putting this construction (which the evidence supports) upon his conduct, I must pronounce him to have violated the engagements which he made when admitted into the order of Deacons, and to have committed such a breach of the ordinances of the Church, at such a time and place, and with so many attendant circumstances of aggravation that all our discipline must be overthrown if such an offence be passed over without receiving a sentence of due severity."

The Bishop then referred to Francis Russell's words to Mr Naylor, "Be candid, Mr Naylor, is not Mr Walsh at the bottom of all this?" Francis Russell's own account of the proceedings asserts that "when the Bishop opened his second charge, I said, 'I am prepared with explanations. Mr Walsh has admitted that he has spoken most improperly of me.' His Lordship, with a menacing gesture, declared if I dared to utter a word he would deprive me of my Orders and charged me on my oath of allegiance not to speak." The Bishop, in his statement, was concerned that Mr Walsh should have been accused of some conspiracy against Francis Russell. Also, that in spite of a most moderate letter to him from Mr Walsh, the other had not indicated how he felt that he had been injured nor had he withdrawn his accusation. "I am therefore compelled, unwillingly to interpose in obtaining for Mr Walsh the vindication to which he is justly entitled. His character as a clergyman is the property of the Church, and I cannot suffer it to be traduced in my presence, and in the presence of others of the clergy, without requiring that the imputation should be no less publicly and explicitly withdrawn. This Mr Russell has omitted or refused to do, and has thus exposed himself to such ecclesiastical censure as shall be suitable to the offence.

Lastly, the Bishop commented on Francis Russell's reply to his questions concerning the existence of a Romanizing clique in the Diocese. After reviewing the evidence that the latter had offered, the Bishop concluded: "I cannot discover or admit that any other statements or arguments offered by Mr Russell can justify the assertion which he has made, that there is among us, at this time, a Romanizing party which has combined to injure him. He does not put it in the way of a question whether or no such a party exists here, but he plainly insinuates the fact. This he could have no right to affirm, unless he were prepared with some kind of evidence. He has had the fullest opportunity afforded him, and has been called upon to produce it. He fails entirely to do so; and deals only in allusions and insinuations, such as cannot always be understood, and still less could they be answered. Sitting now in judgement upon Mr Russell's conduct, I must express my persuasion that it has been altogether unjustifiable. This last charge I said was the most important of all, and this is my decided opinion.

"I repeat an observation already offered, that the constant repetition of statements without foundation, casting discredit upon the Church, is one of the most serious offences which a clergyman can be guilty of, as it gives rise to suspicions which destroy all confidence among the members of the Church, and prevent the possibility of their acting together for the general benefit. This offence must therefore weigh with me in the sentence which I have now to pronounce; indeed, I may declare that it alone would justify such a degree of punishment, even if the other two charges were left entirely out of consideration." The Bishop then went on to deliver his judgement, without giving Francis Russell any opportunity to speak, as had been promised in the Archdeacon's letter of the 23rd July. This action was entirely justified in the eyes of four of the clergymen who were present. They later wrote to the Bishop, "... we considered his deportment most discourteous, not to say positively offensive; and we distinctly heard him repeatedly ejaculate, 'that is false', 'that is totally untrue' and the like, during the delivery of your Lordship's charge, which appeared to us grossly insulting. Such conduct, we conceive, cancelled any expectation which Mr Russell may have had of being personally heard at that time; and we felt relieved when you arose to leave the Court immediately; after pronouncing the sentence." One of those who signed this letter was the Rev. W. H. Walsh of Christ Church.

"The sentence is—That the Reverend F. T. C. Russell be suspended *ab officio* for the space of three months from this day, and be inhibited from discharging any of the offices of a Deacon during that time, and until he shall have made to me satisfactory acknowledgement of his fault."

In this way the court held in the Vestry at St. James' was concluded and that evening Francis Russell received the following letter.

Sydney. 25th July, 1849

REVEREND SIR,

By direction of the Lord Bishop of Sydney, I herewith transmit to you a copy of the sentence of suspension *ab officio* passed upon you by his Lordship this day; and I am instructed to inform you that his Lordship passed this sentence in support of the discipline of the Church which you have violated and in maintenance of his authority.

At the same time, as has been already intimated to you, I am to inform you that, if after having heard the grounds of his Lordship's decision, you desire to offer any observations—to make any concessions—or to urge any reasons why the sentence should be, in any respect, reconsidered, I am directed to be in attendance at the vestry of St. James's Church, at 10 o'clock A. M., on Monday next, to receive from you any statement you may make in writing, and to convey the same to the Bishop of Sydney for his consideration.

I am, Reverend Sir,
Your most obedient servant,

J. NORTON
Registrar.

Rev. F. T. C. Russell, B.A.

(Enclosure)

At a court holden this twenty-fifth day of July, one thousand eight hundred and forty-nine, before the Right Reverend William Grant, Lord Bishop of Sydney, and Metropolitan, in the vestry of St. James's Church, in the City of Sydney,

It was ordered,

That the Reverend Francis Thomas Cusack Russell, B.A., Deacon, licensed Minister of the Parish of St. Mark, Alexandria, in the Diocese of Sydney, for certain infractions of the discipline of the Church of England, declared to him by the Right Reverend William Grant, Bishop of Sydney, and Metropolitan, to have been duly proved, be, in accordance with the Canons of the Church, suspended *ab officio*; and be inhibited from the discharge of the duties of a deacon, for the space of three calendar months from the 25th day of July, 1849, and until he shall have made satisfactory acknowledgement of his fault to the said Bishop.

J. NORTON

Registrar of the Diocese of Sydney.

Chapter Nine

In consequence of the notice given in the letter from the Registrar of the Diocese that that official would receive any submissions that Francis Russell might care to make, the latter entered a solemn protest against the sentence which had been pronounced by the Bishop. In doing this he had to rely on his own recollection of the events and a report which was published in the Sydney Morning Herald on 26th July. He had applied to the Registrar and to the Bishop's Secretary for a copy of the Bishop's written judgement, but this request was refused. The reply from the Bishop's Secretary was as follows.

Sydney, 30th July, 1849

REVEREND SIR,

Having submitted to the Bishop of Sydney your note of the 28th *inst*, wherein you desire to be furnished with a copy of the statement read by his Lordship in the Vestry of St. James's, on Wednesday last, the 25th instant, I am instructed to inform you that his Lordship considers your conduct on the occasion to have debarred yourself from any right to make application to him on any subject, and he therefore must decline to comply with your application.

I remain.
Reverend Sir.
Your most obedient servant,

H. KERRISON JAMES.

Rev. F. T. C. Russell

Francis Russell began, "I, Francis T. Cusack Russell, Clerk, Bachelor of Arts, of Trinity College, in the University of Dublin, do most solemnly protest against the sentence of suspension pronounced by the Right Rev. William Grant Broughton, D.D., Lord Bishop of Sydney, and Metropolitan..." In this document he deals point by point with the matters raised in the prepared statement read by the Bishop before he pronounced his sentence. His position is shown clearly in the summary with which his protest concluded.

"I respectfully submit that the sentence pronounced ought not to be recorded.

1. Because it is evident from the judgement read by the Lord Bishop of Sydney, that such sentence was founded upon certain charges never before made known to me in any shape, or at any rate under a totally different form.

"2. Because by letter dated 13th July, from Archdeacon Cowper, conveying to me the Bishop's instructions to him, the charge upon which sentence was to be pronounced, and to which I was invited to reply, differs widely from those brought against me on the 25th of July, upon which sentence was pronounced.

"3. Because up to the 23rd July, I had no knowledge that the first or second charges were to be preferred against me at all.

"4. Because until sentence was being pronounced, the charges in the form they now bear were entirely concealed from me.

"5. Because the charges attributed motives to me which never actuated me; which I had disavowed, and which were alleged upon suspicion only.

"6. Because the judgement assumes certain facts to be proven, of which no or insufficient proofs were offered.

"7. Because it is alleged that I used expressions and made statements in writing, when I deny that I ever did, and of which no proofs have been offered.

"8. Because no notice was given to me that witnesses were to be examined against me, or opportunity allowed me of cross-examination.

"9. Because, when I succeeded, in the face of great impediments, in proving that I had good grounds for asserting my belief that there existed in this diocese a Romanizing party, a point which I was called upon, under penalty, to establish; I was held to have failed in my proof because I did not also show that such clique or party had conspired to debar me from the priesthood, a point which I had not asserted, and of which I was not required to offer proofs.

"10. Because, although I received from Archdeacon Cowper, notice, by direction of the Bishop of Sydney, that before sentence should be passed I was to be permitted to make explanations or concessions, yet when I respectfully professed my readiness to enter upon my defence, I was peremptorily refused a hearing...

"For these and other weighty reasons, for the welfare of the Church, for the honor of the sacred ministry, I, with all humility do submit, that the sentence pronounced is not in accordance with the principles of the British Constitution, with the rules of equity and right reason, with the laws of the land, with the canons ecclesiastical, or with the holy precepts of the Christian faith.

"And, therefore, ought forthwith to be revoked."

This statement was considered by the Bishop but nothing in it moved him from his decision delivered on the 25th July, and on the 6th August he confirmed the sentence of suspension.

"Having pronounced the preceding sentence upon the Rev. F. T. C. Russell, I made reservation to him of opportunity to offer, within a time limited, any concessions and explanations, and to urge any grounds why the same should be reconsidered. Certain written statements, in connexion therewith, have been submitted by him in accordance with the above reservation. In substance, Mr Russell was charged with a profanation of the Church by exhibiting writings and using words within it, indicative of personal revenge and animosity, and with injuring its character by affirming in print the existence of "a Romanizing clique", and "an unprincipled party," to whom he attributes by implication that they had combined to debar him from his priesthood.

"Upon an attentive review of the explanations which he has tendered, I do not find that they satisfactorily refute these charges; nor do they contain any due acknowledgement of the extreme sinfulness of his conduct in the above respects. I have therefore, upon such review, and bearing in mind the solemn account which I must render to God for every judgement of mine as presiding in His Church, pronounced the charges to be fully proved; and do confirm accordingly the preceding sentence of suspension and inhibition against the Rev. F. T. C. Russell, trusting only that he may yet render null and supercede the same by due submission, and acknowledgement of his fault.

"Given under my hand, at Sydney, this sixth day of August, in the year of our Lord one thousand eight hundred and forty-nine.

W. G. SYDNEY"

This decision was conveyed to Francis Russell in a letter from the Registrar dated 10th August.

REVEREND SIR,

I am commanded by the Lord Bishop of Sydney to inform you, that he has carefully perused and considered the statements you conveyed to him through me, and that he sees no reason to depart from the terms of the sentence of suspension and inhibition pronounced by his Lordship on the 25th *ultimo*, and that he has therefore been pleased to confirm the same.

To this sentence you have, of course, the right of appeal to His Grace the Archbishop of Canterbury.

I have the honor to be,
Reverend Sir,
Your most obedient Servant,

J. NORTON Registrar.

The parishioners of Alexandria North to whom Francis Russell had ministered for almost two years had been most concerned for him during this time. We have already seen that two of them had approached the Bishop on his behalf and that a number of them had been present in the Vestry at St. James' Church on the day of the trial. When it was known that he had been sentenced by the Bishop the following Address was presented to him signed by eighty of the people of the parish, on the 2nd August.

TO THE REV. F. T. C. RUSSELL. B.A.

REVEREND SIR,

We, the undersigned Parishioners of Alexandria (North), and others, who have attended your Ministry in the temporary Chapel of St. Mark, in that Parish, have heard with extreme sorrow that the Lord Bishop of Sydney has thought proper to suspend you for three months from the performance of your duties as a Minister of the Church of England, which suspension is coupled with conditions that may for a further period deprive us of your ministerial services.

In consequence of this painful occurrence. we are anxious to convey to you, as early as possible. our sincere appreciation of your zealous efforts to promote the spiritual welfare of the Parish, the good efforts of which are distinctly visible; and at the same time to declare the respect and esteem which we all cannot but entertain towards you, whether we regard the sincerity and sound doctrine displayed in your ministrations in the Church, the innocency of your private life and conversation, or your unremitting attentions to the indigent and the afflicted, to the aged and the youthful members of the flock hitherto entrusted to your care.

With sincere feelings of gratitude for your past exertions, and of interest in your future welfare, we earnestly desire to be made acquainted with the offences laid to your charge, with the defence which you were enabled to offer, and, if possible, with the judgement delivered by the Lord Bishop of Sydney, in order that we may know the whole of the circumstances which have induced his Lordship to pronounce so severe a condemnation upon one whom we unite in regarding as a faithful Minister of the Gospel.

W. DUMARESQ

M. BLANCENBERG

J. PATRICK

and seventy-seven others.

Francis Russell wrote a reply to this Address from the parishioners in a letter dated 3rd August 1849.

MY DEAR FRIENDS AND BRETHREN IN CHRIST,

Accept my heartfelt thanks for the kind expression of sympathy your address conveys.

I cannot appropriate, for I am sensible (God knows how sensible) that I do not merit the commendatory terms in which you mention my feeble efforts for the spiritual welfare of those committed to my care.

But sometimes the language of exaggeration is natural and allowable; and, no doubt, the present troubles with which you see me compassed, have hid from your eyes my manifold failings and shortcomings.

Whilst your pastor, I sought to "know nothing among you save Jesus Christ, even Him crucified;" as God's ambassador, I endeavoured to make known the "riches of His mercy in Christ Jesus" our Saviour, the author and finisher of our faith, who giveth repentance as well as forgiveness of sins; who delivereth his people not only from the condemnation but from the dominion of sin.

Nor have my labours been altogether vain, God has not withheld a blessing upon His own means; some have believed, even to the salvation of their souls.

Full of pain, then, to me is the interruption to our connexion; but let us feel sure that "all things work together for good to them that love God." "God doth not afflict willingly, nor grieve the children of men."

It is only your right, and is clearly my duty to comply with your request, that you should be "made acquainted with the offences laid to my charge, and with the defence I was enabled to offer."

And now, brethren, dearly beloved, whether the time of our separation be long or short, let us acquiesce with thankfulness in the will of God; let us with one mind unite in prayer for the welfare of the Church of England.

The signs of the times are neither few nor indistinct. May our Protestant and evangelical Church give forth no uncertain note of preparation for the coming struggle; that her sons clad in the panoply of the Gospel, armed with the sword of the Spirit, which is the word of God, under the great Captain of our salvation, may earnestly contend for the faith once for all delivered to the saints.

Praying that the peace of God may for ever abide with you, and that of his great mercy he will vouchsafe that he who preached to you be not himself a cast-away.

I remain,
Your affectionate friend in Christ Jesus,

F. T. CUSACK RUSSELL, Clerk, B.A..

Of Trinity College, Dublin.

During the following fortnight the various documents which related to his suspension were collected by T. Whistler Smith and eventually published in the pamphlet *Statement of the Rev. F. T. C. Russell, B.A..* The only serious omission was a copy of the Bishop's Judgement which was read before the sentence of suspension was pronounced. However this was soon available to the public in a pamphlet published in order to present the official position, entitled *Report of the Proceedings in the case of the Rev. F. T. C. Russell...* which also contained an appendix of relevant documents. The last letter contained in the Statement is one written by Francis Russell to the Reverend W. H. Walsh, M.A..

REVEREND SIR,

When your friend, the Rev. T. Druitt, conveyed to me your letter of the 30th last, I desired (as you mentioned that it was merely for your own satisfaction you sought a reply) to return a verbal answer; this Mr Druitt refused receiving.

As I had promised my legal adviser to abstain from all correspondence upon subjects in the least connected with a matter at that time pending, I was not at liberty to do more, and this I explained to your friend.

I have now to state that you acknowledged to me the truth of statements published in the *Sydney Chronicle*, (of 10th June, 1848) to the effect that you had, where I had no opportunity of defence, taxed me with heresy.

I desire to express my regret for having asked Mr Naylor, in the vestry of St. Andrew's Church— "Whether Mr Walsh was his informant?" and also, for having used your name in my letters, published in the *Sydney Herald*.

Reverend Sir,
I remain,
Your obedient Servant,

F. T. CUSACK RUSSELL

St. Mark's, Sydney, August 15th, 1849.

Chapter Ten

Francis Russell did not prolong his residence in Sydney. Before the close of 1849 he had moved to Melbourne with his wife Margaret and his friend Peter Beamish. He was not, however, forgotten by his former parishioners. "A testimonial of 500 pounds, with which they presented him on leaving, was an inadequate expression of the esteem in which they held him, and of the affection which they cherished towards him"

The first Bishop of Melbourne, the Right Rev'd Charles Perry, had arrived in that city at the end of January 1848. Before his arrival there were only three clergymen in the area of his new Diocese, and the only one in the area to the west of Geelong was the Rev'd James Yelverton Wilson, who had been at Portland since June 1842. After his arrival, one of Bishop Perry's first concerns was to learn at first hand the needs of country people. He first visited Gippsland and then before the year was out he was visiting the Western District. We have vivid descriptions of most of these journeys from the pen of Mrs Perry who was always with her husband on these expeditions.

Here is an extract from one of her letters which describes their first visit to Portland: — "Portland is a pretty village very nicely situated on a small bay, which is too open to the sea to afford good anchorage in stormy weather. The cliff, half rock, half earth— the earth being the higher part— is covered with a variety of shrubs, and at this season [November] many wild flowers, but nothing very pretty... The great draw back to the place is, that it is so entirely shut in on the land side by dense forests of gum and stringy bark; the road through which is so swampy, that no carriage can traverse it at present. Owing to this I was obliged to my great disappointment to remain behind, while Charles, accompanied by Rev. J. Y. Wilson and a mounted policeman, whom Captain Dana most kindly placed at our disposal, rode sixty miles up the country to attend a meeting relating to church matters at the River Wannon."

THE RIGHT REVD CHARLES PERRY, FIRST BISHOP OF MELBOURNE

From a photograph by Antoine Fauchery, ca 1858:
Pictures Collection, State Library of Victoria, H84.167/17

If this visit was concerned with the appointment of a clergyman in the Wannon area, it was not until a year later that the transfer of Francis Russell and Peter Beamish from Sydney to Melbourne made it possible for the Bishop to take action in the matter. Before the end of 1849 Francis Russell and his friend were visiting the homes of some of the squatters in the District of the Wannon with whom, no doubt, they were concerned to come to an arrangement for the accommodation of their new Parson. I suppose that there were many different reactions to the proposed settling of a Parson in the district. One of those whom they visited was John H. Jackson at Sandford Station who in later years said, "I recollect thinking that we had got along very well without a parson up to that time, and wondered what we wanted with one, I little thought that I was to become his faithful adherent and admirer to the extent that I did in the years that were to come."

The Registrar's Book of the Diocese of Melbourne sets out the formal details of Francis Russell's appointment. "The Reverend Francis Thomas Cusack Russell appeared before the Bishop of Melbourne and exhibited his Letters of Orders as a Deacon on 14th June 1850 and was then licensed for ministerial duty in the Wannon area." So in that same month he set out for the Wannon district accompanied by his wife and his old friend Peter Beamish who had been appointed to Warrnambool. The last named has given us a description of their journey to their new home.

"In the month of June in that year [1850] a company of three left on horse-back the hospitable home of the Rev. Francis Hales of Heidelberg (now Archdeacon Hales of Launceston) and journeying first to Melbourne, proceeded thence by steam-boat to Geelong taking their horses with them... From Geelong they travelled westward by long stages, passing the nights at bush inns, which had been erected along the route, or at settlers' houses. More than once as they journied, weary and benighted, they looked forward wistfully into the darkness hoping to discern the light of the inn at which they should find rest and refreshment. At Lake Bolac station, where they were hospitably entertained by Mr Peterson, Mr and Mrs Russell parted from their friend who turned southward towards the sea coast, while they still held their way westward until they reached one of the valleys of the Wannon."

At first the Russells probably stayed at the various stations in the district. There were as yet no church buildings and most services would be held at the various homesteads and at the local inns. An indication of this is given in the records of baptisms and weddings performed in the district in 1850. In August there was a baptism at Glenelg and a marriage at Sandford. In September a baptism at Lewis' Inn Emu Creek (Co. Normanby). In October there were baptisms at Upper Glenelg, Sandford and Merino Downs and in December marriages at Sandford, Merino Downs and Violet Creek and baptisms at Tahara, Wilton Upper Wannon, Spring Vale and Burton on the Wannon. Sandford, Merino Downs and Tahara were all sheep stations whose names have been perpetuated in the district.

In 1851 it is recorded that the marriage of William Morris a shoemaker and Mary Anne Morris a widow was celebrated at the Parsonage on the Wannon. This ceremony was described in the opening chapter of this book, but it is also the first recorded event which took place at the Parsonage. The Parsonage was situated centrally in the district but was not in any of the developing townships of the area. The land on which it stood comprises 100 acres beside the Wannon River not far from the present Coleraine-Merino Road. This land was bought by Francis Russell himself at a land sale in Hamilton, but he was reimbursed later by the efforts of Samuel Pratt Winter (Murndal), John Coldham (Grassdale), John McConochie (Konongwootong Creek). J. H. Jackson (Sandford House), and George Robertson (Warrock). The Parsonage was built by Samuel Pratt Winter and an east wing was later added by his brother-in-law Cecil Pybus Cooke, the two sections "being connected by a planked, bark-roofed, trellis-walled passage." It is still possible to see where the house stood, the spot being marked by some trees, remains of foundations and an underground tank.

There must have once been quite an extensive garden. In a note to a friend visiting Melbourne (probably S. P. Winter) Francis Russell wrote— "Should you be purchasing any trees I should like 2 Walnuts, 2 Spanish Chestnuts, 2 Mulberry, 2 Blackheart Cherries, 2 Nectarines and any others you think would do well with me, I have room for about 16 trees." Dr Ernest S. Jackson many years later remembered the garden and its attractions. He tells of Kentish Cherry trees, a double row of Oleanders and the central path going down through the garden from the front steps of the house.

In the 1960s the Parsonage land still belonged to the church and it provided an income for the clergyman in whose parish it was situated. The wording of the trust deed which was to provide for this was apparently the subject of a letter written in 1872 by Francis Russell to a young friend who was with a

FRANCIS RUSSELL & THE PARSONAGE GARDEN

From a painting by Pain based on a photograph.

legal firm in Melbourne. "I have a nut for you to crack & consider yourself before the Master of the Bench on a gaudy-day at 'Moots'. — T. Z. wishes to confer a gift of land to the parson of X Victoria to be held by him and his successors in the cure of souls. The difficulties in the way are 1st the parson of X is not a corporation sole 2nd the definition of a "clergyman of the C of England in Victoria" 3rd that the objects of donor would be defeated were his land alienated or enjoyed by one not conformable to the doctrine, discipline, worship & ritual of Church of England..."

He then went on to outline a suggestion made by the Registrar of the Diocese, raised a few difficulties and went on to make some suggestions of his own. The result was described by Ada Cambridge the wife of the Reverend George Cross who was the successor of Francis Russell in the Wannon area. "It is an inalienable endowment, not to any parish—for there was none—but to the incumbent for the time being; so that afterwards, when it came to belong to a parish, whose centre of town and church was six miles off, the vestry could not turn it into money, as they desired, so as to bring their parson to head quarters."

Travel at first was on horseback and Dr Jackson had memories of the Parson's horses "all with a dash, or more than that, of Arab blood. There was 'Molly Bawn' and 'Mermaid', 'Hassim' and 'Sybil' who belonged to Miss Smithson." Even when Bishop Perry visited the district travel was on horseback. These days we do not always appreciate the difficulties which this involved. For example, the thirty kilometres from Digby to Sandford are now a pleasant drive over rolling country along a well-made road. But compare this with a description from a summary of the Bishop's tour in 1862.

"April 25— left Portland with the Rev. Dr. Russell for the district of the Wannon and Glenelg; slept that evening at Hotspur, formerly known as Smoky River. Conducted short service in school-room.

"April 26— Started early for Digby, where breakfasted, and afterwards proceeded by Merino to Sandford; a long and heavy journey, in the course of which the horses gave strong indications of jibbing and finally came to a stand still at the foot of the last hill."

Because Francis Russell covered such a wide area in providing pastoral care for the people of the district, arrangements had to be made to notify him of any cases of urgent need.

There still stands an old Red-Gum tree on the road to Tahara which was used as a letter-box where messages could be left for him.

At Coleraine where there was the nucleus of a town, he had a different method of finding where his presence was needed. "When Dr. Russell would come into Coleraine it was always his practice to pull up in front of Trangmar's store. After bidding the time of day he would ask, 'Are there any sick in the Township?' If the reply was 'Yes' he would go to them immediately; if 'No', he would put his horse up at Mr Trangmar's stable, feed it, and then have some refreshments."

But all this time spent in the saddle did affect his physical condition. In October 1859 he wrote to Peter Beamish. "I have a constant pain along the course of the Ischiatic nerve, and am beginning to be conscious of a distaste for horseback, but yet I would be no denison of a town." By 1872, at the latest, he had exchanged the saddle for a buggy and in that year had one made to his own specifications.

Melbourne, 29th May. 1872

My Dear Dr. Russell,

I hope you will excuse my not answering your note sooner, as I have been very much engaged during the last few days. I have however seen Craine, I told him what you wish to have done regarding the buggy. He does not think that it would be desirable to use Collins' patent axles, which he says cannot be relied upon as sound in this country, but recommends adhering to the original plan of using the English Mail Axle which as you know is on the same principle as Collins. All your other instructions I have given him in writing, as well as those sent by Mr Winter, & shall from time to time call at Craine's works to see that they are properly carried out. The buggy was commenced on last Monday 27th. I have suggested that the cushions & lining be dark blue, as drab soils so easily, but if you prefer the latter please let me know.

Please remember me very kindly to Mrs Russell & Miss Smithson, and with kind regards from Mrs Kerr.

Believe me
Yours very sincerely,
John Hunter Kerr

Chapter Eleven

In the Year Book of the Diocese of Melbourne for 1864 we find the following information about the District of the Wannon.

Centre	Building	Accommodation	Number at main service	Number of services a year	Sunday School Teachers	Sunday School Pupils
Coleraine	School-house	120	120	12	5	37
Muntham	School-house	30	-	12	-	-
Casterton	School-house	120	120	13	3	40
Digby	Church	200	-	28	3	63
Merino	Chapel	180	-	28	3	56
Sandford	School-house	35	-	12	3	38
District	Various Private Houses					

As you can see, the church at Digby was the first to be erected. No doubt the local people had been encouraged by the work of Mr R. J. Mercer, a stipendiary Lay Reader who was resident there. However there were initial problems in financing the building. "It has for some time past been the anxious desire of the inhabitants of Digby, to erect on the township a building for public worship in connexion with the Church of England, but want of money has hitherto prevented them accomplishing their wishes. However, during the last month, the unwearied efforts of Dr. Russell to obtain 300 pounds from the Bishop, having been crowned with success, coupled with a munificent donation from a gentleman in the neighbourhood, have somewhat changed the state of affairs, and we are now in a fair way to see a neat and commodious church occupying the site so long vacant." The foundation stone was laid by Francis Russell on Friday 19th April 1861 at a service commencing at midday. In his address he spoke to those present of the "duty and happiness of devoting a certain portion of their income to the service of God. He showed how important it was to make due provision for the public ordinances of religion, without which the spiritual life languishes and dies out of the soul." He also stressed the importance of religion to the good health of the community and expressed concern for "the generation bred up beyond the sound of the church-going bell".

"It was not so much speculative infidelity he feared, as practical disregard of religion arising from thoughtlessness, and the common temptations of life; hence, it is absolutely necessary that the forms of religion should be kept up with due reverence, otherwise, from living in forgetfulness of God, men will at length cease to believe in Him and so sink down into stupid brutish atheism. In the bosom of society there are many forces at work to rive it asunder. Men are separated into various ranks, one section looking down

ST JOHN'S CHURCH, DIGBY

with disdain upon another, and the latter rendering back hate for scorn, feeling that–

> "Rank is but the guinea stamp,
> Man is the goud for a' that."

"Now unless religion be allowed to bind up the wounds no human legislation, no furious assertions of equality and fraternity can do so; the causes of irritation will still rankle, and the whole body politic become gangrened. But, under the mild influences of religion, all asperities are softened; rich and poor, the high born and the lowly, the learned and the simple, are taught their several duties. In the house of God all distinctions are levelled; there they address one Father, do homage to one common Redeemer, and seek to partake of the same immortal blessedness."

The Chapel at Merino was also erected at this time (although it was to be replaced within a few years). However the construction of these first two church buildings was not achieved without difficulty, mostly arising, it would seem from Francis Russell's reluctance to conform with the procedures set down by the Diocesan Authorities. In a letter written to Samuel Pratt Winter of 11 May 1861 he complained "...I wrote to the Bp. at great length on the Grants and endeavoured to impress upon them (Bp. and Council) that delays would hurt us as rejection.

"It was just as I thought, the Dioc. Architect condemned the plans because no proper plans were set before him— He of course ignored the rough draft as not done by a professional hand. At least I gather so much from the Bps letter. I shall be in a disagreeable position if these delays be continued much longer. Indeed hardly ever have I had to conduct a correspondence with the School Board that I did not frame the resolve to have nought more to do with school buildings and the Bp. & Co. seem as impracticable.

"I have over & over stated

1. that the Church or Chapel at Digby & at Merino are built on sites granted by the Crown for Churches.

2. The trustees are elected according to the act.

3. The plans are sufficient in accommodation for the outlay and sound in their principles of construction; Merino being a copy of a Board of Ordnance

THE INTERIOR OF ST JOHN'S, DIGBY

School house, Digby by Mr. Barrow who writes himself Architect & C. Engineer.

4. The subscriptions are finnisht according to regulats.

5. The buildings are nearly up and instalments to builders overdue.

"That we adopted this course without awaiting the issue of a correspondence was necessary if we wished to have the buildings erected at all. Soon the weather is so broken that neither brick could be made or timber carted from the forest."

In spite of all these difficulties the building at Digby was finished by the end of the year, although there was still plastering and furnishing to be done. St John's was opened on Sunday 8 December 1861 at a service conducted by Dr Russell. His friend from Warrnambool, Dr P. T Beamish preached, taking as his text Matthew 26:6ff, the story of the woman with the alabaster box of very precious ointment which she poured on Jesus' head. Very likely he laid some stress on Jesus' reply to the criticism that the woman should have sold the ointment and given the proceeds to help the poor. "For ye have the poor always with you; but me ye have not always." There was a practical response to his preaching as the sum of £21 was collected at the conclusion of the service.

The correspondent to the *Hamilton Spectator* after describing the opening had this to say— "The residents of Digby have been anxiously looking forward for the completion of their church, which the severe winter has retarded; but their patience has been amply rewarded by Sunday's impressive services and by the universal admiration which the interior and exterior appearance of the building elicited. The church stands on the hill, and can be seen from a great distance. When plastered and completely furnished, it will be second to none in the district. We believe the trustees intend petitioning the Bishop to consecrate it during his next visit to the Wannon."

The church at Digby was finally completed in July 1863 and this description appeared in *The Church Gazette*: "The Church of St. John the Evangelist was re-opened, on the 14th *inst*., for public worship, by the Rev. Dr. Russell, clergyman of the district... The Church has been closed for two months, in order that the walls might be plastered, the seats, &c., stained and varnished; and the Lord's Prayer, the Apostles' Creed, the Decalogue, and the Beatitudes, written upon the ornamental tablets prepared for the purpose; the whole of the work (except the last named portion) is completed, and the manner in which it has been executed is deserving of the highest praise; the walls, especially the east end, are adorned with most elaborate enrichments and have been universally admired. The Chancel (which is divided from the body of the church by a massive and elaborate rail) is provided with a beautiful cedar Communion Table, having a rich crimson cloth, with the Monogram in gold, it has also two carved Fald Stools, and the floor is covered with Brussels carpet of appropriate pattern. The Lectern at which the lessons are read is a copy of the one in use at the Sydney University, but as soon as funds permit it will be superceded by a carved Eagle as being more appropriate. The windows at the east end will shortly be filled with stained glass, the designs for which have been supplied by a Melbourne firm, and are exceedingly neat and rich. The above is a brief description of the first building exclusively devoted to the public worship of God, erected in Dr. Russell's district, but it is confidently anticipated that, in a year or two, each township at which that devoted gentleman officiates will be similarly privileged."

This confident prediction was in good part fulfilled. By 1866, after a great deal of building activity, there were churches at Coleraine, Merino and Casterton as well as Digby. Services were also held in the Schoolhouse at Sandford, Gumbuck, Muntham and Hotspur. Work began on the churches at Coleraine and Merino in 1865. Tenders for the Coleraine church were invited in advertisements in the *Hamilton Spectator* in January and for the Merino church at the beginning of February. Then on Wednesday 8 February the following item appeared in that paper:

COLERAINE—We omitted in our last issue to draw attention to the ceremony of laying the foundation stone of the Episcopal Church about to be erected at Coleraine, which is to take place today. The Church, which is designed and will be superintended in the building by Mr. Fox, of Hamilton, is to be entirely of stone, and when completed will comprise a nave with a clear story, a south aisle, porch, chansel [sic], vestry, and tower. The Church, of which Dr. Russell is the pastor, is dedicated to the Holy Trinity. At the same time the annual gathering of the children in connection with the school will take place, when several prizes will be given and a feast provided for the occasion.

In the next issue of the paper on Saturday 11 February 1865 quite a full report of the proceedings was printed. Here is how their reporter described the scene, and the ceremonies.

COLERAINE (from our own correspondent)

This quiet and picturesque little township on Wednesday last, was the scene of life and gaiety, in consequence of that day being the anniversary of the gathering of the children of the neighbourhood, and the double event of it being appointed for the laying of the foundation stone of the new church. From an early hour in the morning, the Union Jack was hoisted to direct the visitors to the site of the new church, where the first ceremony was to take place. About one o'clock. the Rev. Dr. Russell commenced by reading a suitable passage from Scripture, after which a prayer was delivered, and the Hundredth Psalm was sung. He then gave a very feeling and impressive address, appropriate to the occasion, at the conclusion of which Mr McConachie, the Treasurer, came forward, and, in the name of the ladies of Coleraine, stated, after a few appropriate remarks, that it was his pleasing duty, to present the reverend gentleman with a silver trowel. (The trowel, which is a beautiful piece off workmanship, and most tastefully got up,

HOLY TRINITY CHURCH, COLERAINE

certainly reflects great credit upon the taste of the donors). After the presentation and the Rev Dr Russell having returned thanks for the handsome gift he had received, the laying of the stone commenced by first placing a bottle in the lower stone, the bottle containing a copy of the *Argus* and *Hamilton Spectator*, sundry coins, and a piece of lead about nine inches long bearing a Latin inscription and on which were the names of His Lordship, Bishop Perry, the Rev. Dr. Russell, the members of the Committee— Messrs. Trangmar, McConachie, and McKebery and the name of the architect. Mr J. H. Fox. After depositing the bottle, the stone was fixed. and declared by Dr Russell to be well and truly laid. The Rev. Dr. Beamish, of Warrnambool, then addressed the meeting, after which another psalm was sung and the ceremony of laying the stone was closed with prayer.

After the conclusion of the above ceremony, the Rev. Dr. Russell gave a general invitation to all present to adjourn to Mr Kerr's paddock. On arriving there, we found extensive preparations had been made for the reception of the numerous guests, who could not have numbered less than 300, this number being exclusive of nearly 300 children, all of whom were now gaily dressed in holiday attire. The ladies, who numbered numerously, were, for the most part splendid specimens of the fair sex, their happy faces and exuberant spirits adding much to the hilarity of the day's amusements, and well may Coleraine be proud of possessing so many bonnie lassies.

Building of the Church went slowly and by the end of 1866 the Nave and Tower had been built. The Architect had intended that the South Aisle and the Porch should also be built leaving only the Chancel and Vestry to be completed later, but this had not been possible. The building as it was cost about 1600 pounds which was provided from Government grants and loans from the Episcopal fund and from Mrs Russell, as well as the donations of parishioners. Finally the following advertisement appeared in the *Hamilton Spectator* on Wednesday 31 October and Saturday 3 November, 1866.

TRINITY CHURCH, COLERAINE

On SUNDAY, the 4th NOVEMBER,1866, DIVINE SERVICE will be held (D.V.) at noon, in the Church of the Most Holy Trinity, Coleraine.

The Holy Communion will be celebrated.

The ALMS of the Congregation will be devoted to the discharge of the Debt on the Church.

The Trustees having resolved that no payment for Sittings or Pew Rents shall be exacted, but that Trinity Church shall be open without charge and without respect of Persons to all who desire to attend Public Worship of GOD, appeal to the Christian feeling and sense of duty of the community to give according as GOD has given to them for the furtherance of His Honor and glory.

F. T. CUSACK RUSSELL Clerk.

By 1866 the churches were completed in Merino and Casterton as well as Digby and Coleraine. The foundation stone of St. Peter's Merino had been laid on Easter Monday, 17 April 1865 and in this account of Francis Russell's address on that occasion we are not only given a description of the building but also some indications of the principles which he thought were important when building a church.

"He traced the successive stages of progress made in establishing the ordinances of religion at Merino, until it was resolved to provide a Church, which would afford room for the seemly and reverent celebration of the Divine offices and stand forth as a memorial of the homage due to God from

SAINT PETER'S CHURCH, MERINO

his creatures. The plans, prepared with much skill and taste by the architect, Mr Fox, shewed a nave 60 feet by 25 feet, with a southern porch, transepts, chancel, and a central tower. The nave complete in itself would suffice for the present, and the further needs of the parish could be met by extensions, without violence to the original design. The characteristic features of a true ecclesiastical edifice were faithfully observed, so that the traveller as he approached Merino and caught sight of St. Peter's, would at first glance recognize it as a Church, and not a little Bethel or a Salem chapel. The details might be meagre, and the style severe, but all was real, and honest and true, being what it pretended to be.

"Dr. Russell spoke very earnestly as to the propriety of a Church having ample space for the decorous worship of God; he thought that people should not be cooped up in narrow pews so that reverence of body became impossible, but in body as in soul they should bend meekly before the Throne of Grace. A church should be open to all alike—rich and poor, high and low. It should not be an assembly-room for a select company—a middle-class luxury—a deposit of some one or other strata of our social system. But, besides this, there was another purpose, it ought to be an outward, visible token, of man's gratitude to God. This holy season admonished them of their deep debt to Him who suffered poverty, humiliation, betrayal, agony, death, that they might have pardon, peace, and blessedness. What a proof of deadness of soul they gave if their hearts did not burn to testify before men and angels their adoration of Him who so loved and gave Himself for them. No doubt love to Christ was best manifested by doing His will, loving one another and comforting the destitute and afflicted; but while these things should be done, why leave the other undone? We are not left to our own surmises here. Once on a time a poor soul whose heaviness gave place to rest and joy in Christ, came where the Lord 'sat at meat', bringing an alabaster-box of ointment, very precious and she broke the box and poured out the odorous ointment on the Saviour. One of the company rebuked the waste. The cost (so he said) had better been given in alms to the poor. Jesus' tender comment was 'Let her alone'. 'She hath wrought a good work. This she hath done shall be told as a memorial of her wheresoever the gospel is preached.'

"It was Judas Iscariot who found fault, and we are distinctly told that he was a thief, and his care of the poor was a pretence. May there not be in our own times the acting over again of this very scene? A full heart, glad to spend and be spent for the Lord Jesus. A bitter critic standing by casting blame upon the zeal shown for the house of the Lord and the offices thereof, suggesting something more Evangelical, plain—cheaper! Raising up objections as a pretext to cover a churlish disinclination to give. A thief because he robs God of what He claims as His due."

Chapter Twelve

As we saw in the table at the beginning of the previous chapter, services in Coleraine and Casterton were held once a month. This was regretted by a correspondent from Casterton writing in the Hamilton Spectator in December 1860. "If there is one thing more than another that the Castertonians require, it is that of a resident minister. We have the pleasure of hearing the Rev. Dr. Russell only once a month. We must say it does not redound much to the credit of the settlers and the community generally, that religious services should be celebrated here only twelve times in the year, and, sometimes not even so often as that." A comment on the position in Coleraine is provided by an exchange in the same paper at the beginning of 1861.

SABBATH DESECRATION AT COLERAINE

A correspondent whom we know to be highly and deservedly esteemed writes us from the vicinity of Coleraine, complaining of the open and disgraceful violation of the day of rest... Our correspondent mentions that last Sunday he witnessed six reapers at work in the township, and a number of cricketers practising their game close to the school-room walls, at the time the Rev. Dr. Russell was preaching within. This is not as it should be, ye men of Coleraine! Public propriety, if not religion, demands a reformation. (Saturday 26 January 1861)

ORIGINAL CORRESPONDENCE

To the Editor of the Spectator.

SIR- Having perceived in your issue of the 26th January, a communication from a correspondent, headed 'Sabbath Desecration at Coleraine'to the effect that on the previous Sunday (which would be the 20th), he observed six reapers at work near the township, and a number of cricketers practising their game close to the walls of the schoolroom during the time the Rev. Dr. Russell was preaching within; now, Mr Editor, we beg to state that your correspondent is wrong, in the first place, in stating that the Rev. Dr. Russell was preaching here on the Sunday alluded to, as he only does so on the first Sunday in each month, which in January fell on the 4th, instead of the 20th, the day your correspondent refers to. As to the reaping we know nothing about g it; but we beg most emphatically to deny the statement, that our cricketers were practising their game outside the school-room during the hours of divine service...

We remain, Sir, your obedient servants.

TWO MEMBERS OF THE COLERAINE CRICKET CLUB.

(Saturday 2nd February 1861)

The problem of arranging more frequent services in the various centres was largely a problem of manpower. What assistance did Francis Russell have in administering his large parish? As we have seen, there was a stipendiary Lay Reader resident at Digby as early as 1861. This was Rigbye Johnson Mercer whose stipend was a total of £100 per annum (half paid by the Diocese, half from local sources) at a time when the Incumbent's stipend was £330 in 1864 and £415/12/- in 1866. The Year Book for 1866 tells us that his duties were concerned with Digby, Merino, Glen Creek and Hotspur. Mr Mercer later studied for the Ministry at Moore College, Sydney and was ordained by the Bishop of Melbourne (Deacon 1872, Priest 1873). He was later Incumbent of St John's Ballarat for 17 years, a Canon of Christ Church Cathedral, Ballarat for many years and also for a short period was Archdeacon of Ballarat.

An additional complication in providing the ministrations of the Church in the district was the fact that Francis Russell himself was not ordained Priest until 27 May 1866, when he was ordained in St James' Cathedral by Bishop Perry. After the events in the Vestry of St Andrew's, Sydney which had prevented him taking this step in 1849 Francis Russell hesitated to present himself even when urged to do so by his Bishop. (Peter Beamish was ordained by Bishop Perry on 31 December 1854.) Peter Beamish wrote later, "The first charge which the Bishop addressed to the clergy in the western districts of his diocese and which he delivered in Portland, deeply affected Frank Russell, and caused him even to doubt if he was worthy to officiate as a Christian minister." In a letter he himself wrote, "I shrink back from ordination; the Bishop arranged for a private ordination on the first Monday in Lent, but at the last moment, I wrote to decline." Peter Beamish continues, "Eventually providential circumstances, combined with the pressure of friends, convinced him that he must no longer hold back, and he was ordained priest on Trinity Sunday, 27th May, 1866."

So for a long time the people of the district had to rely on visiting clergy for celebrations of the Holy Communion. These would have included the Revd J. Y. Wilson from Portland, the Revd Duncan McKenzie stationed at the Grange (present day Hamilton) in 1855 and his successor from 1856, the Revd Thomas Heron. the Bishop also toured the area from time to time, for example in 1858, 1860, 1862 and 1865. Here is an extract from the *Church Gazette* outlining part of the Bishop's tour in 1862.

April 25— left Portland with the Rev. Dr. Russell for the district of the Wannon and Glenelg; slept that evening at Hotspur, formerly known as Smokey River. Conducted short service in school room.

1 April 26— Started early for Digby, where breakfasted, and afterwards proceeded by Merino to Sandford; a long and heavy journey, in the course of which the horses gave strong indications of jibbing, and fmally came to a stand still at the foot of the last hill.

Sunday, April 27— In the morning preached, and administered the Lord's Supper in the school-room at Casterton, about three miles distant. Evening, preached at Sandford.

April 28— Mr. Jackson, his kind host, having, at some inconvenience to himself, most charitably lent a horse, the Bishop proceeded, still accompanied by Dr. Russell, to Mr G. Robertson's beautiful station; the roads were very sandy, and there was great difficulty in getting the horses through.

April 29— Detained at Mr. Robertson's in consequence of a horse, which he kindly offered to lend, having got out of the paddock.

April 30— With two borrowed horses to Mooree, seven miles from Harrow, the station of Mr. E. Willis. Found that Rev. Mr. Copeland had gone to Apsley to await Bishop's arrival there; but impossible to proceed thither and return in time for service, which he (the Bishop) had engaged to hold at Harrow on Sunday; he was therefore obliged to remain at Mooree.

Sunday, May 4— Moming service at Mooree; afternoon service at Harrow to which Mr. W. kindly drove the Bishop in his buggy.

May 6- With the help of two horses, lent by Mr. Willis, reached Muntham, the station of Mr. E. Henty, where he held evening service.

May 7— Borrowed another horse, and reached Coleraine, where preached, and afterwards drove with Dr. and Mrs Russell to their parsonage, six miles distant.

May 8— Again preached at Coleraine, and administered the Lord's Supper.

May 9— Left the Parsonage with Dr. and Mrs Russell for Digby.

May 10— Preached at Digby in the morning, in the new church, the interior of which is fitted up with great taste and propriety, and does great credit to a resident in the parish, who is never weary in well-doing. In the afternoon preached at Merino, in the school-room; and in the evening at Merino Downs, the station of Mr. F. Henty. A tedious and vexatious conflict with unwilling horses effectually prevented this Sabbath being a day of rest to the party.

May 12— At Merino Downs, again kindly helped with horses, whereby enabled to reach Murndal, the station of Mr. S. Winter, for the night.

May 13— Proceeded to Hamilton...

By the seventies Francis Russell had two assistant curates, but there had been at least one earlier. In July 1870 he wrote, "I have not written to you about Mr Yorke who has been associated with me in this parish for the past half year. He was partly educated at Marlboro' and afterwards at Pembroke Coll Oxford. When ordained he held a curacy in Oxfordshire & there suffered from bleeding (as was supposed) from the lungs. He has a feeble look & wants hardihood of character, but he has found great benefit from his stay on the Wannon. For four years previously he had taken no clerical duty & had acquired the soft ways of an invalid, watchful of his symptoms & careful for his ease. He thinks of leaving for Echuca, hearing that the winter climate of the Murray was best for his case. The Bp. expects a Mr. Cross of S. Augustine's College Canterbury & proposes to send him up here. I am most anxious to keep up the services & extend them, but I can hardly go on doing as I have done with Mr Yorke. From me he receives £50 a year & he lives besides at the Parsonage. This I find causes much trouble & dissatisfaction. The servants complain & Mr Yorke is a man of lazy habits, never once during the six months being up for breakfast, & the flavour of her first trial of a clerical inmate has set my wife's teeth on edge & she decidedly objects to another. So that the successor of Mr Yorke must find a lodging somewhere near Casterton & then I fear £150 will be found insufficient. This drawback of late-rising away Mr Yorke conducts himself with much propriety & good feeling. He wants alertness of mind & is from indolence an assenter, but in an inmate this is far better than a disputatious character.

“He has gone on very well, not equal to much duty, rather from timidity about health, than from positive illness & in the steady work of a well organized Parish he wd. go well. He is not cast in the robust mould and for the rough ways of the colony."

A few years later the Russells met Mr Yorke again in England. By then he had adopted a life at sea as a naval Chaplain as being best for his health. Francis Russell wrote in August 1875, “We were with Yorke, who poor fellow had a bleeding from the lung, but is better, but his stay on land seems to be perilous for him, whereas at sea he is always well. You would like to see the zeal and earnest attention to his duty & the liking of blue jackets & officers & all for him on the *Crocodile*.”

Mr Cross did not take the place of Mr Yorke, but went to Wangaratta in 1870 and then to Yackandandah. However, he did come to the now reduced Parish of the Wannon as Dr Russell’s successor in 1877. In 1872 the Revd W. Kennedy Brodribb came to the Wannon and the Rev’d John Horton Macfarlane was also an assistant from 1873 to 1877. The latter apparently resided in the Casterton area for he became Incumbent of the new Parish of Casterton in 1879 and remained there until 1894, while the former went from the district in 1875 and was at Francis Russell’s old parish of St Mark’s, Sydney in 1877.

Chapter Thirteen

Although most of his time was spent in ministering to the people of the district of the Wannon, Francis Russell did have some contacts with the wider church in the Diocese. Considering the way his relationships with the Bishop and other clergy had deteriorated in the two years that he was in Sydney, how well did he get on with his contemporaries in the Diocese of Melbourne? Canon H. H. P. Handley wrote in an Obituary published in the Church of England Messenger in April 1876, "But it is not only by his personal friends and his parishioners that his death is mourned; it will be felt to be a loss to the whole church; for whether men agreed or not with his opinions, I all acknowledged that he was a power in the councils of the church, and that there was a deference which his deliberate utterances always commanded. Few men exercised a greater influence in the Church Assembly than that which partisans and opponents alike recognized as coming from his conduct."

Francis Russell would have regarded himself as a Churchman according to the standard of the Book of Common Prayer and did not countenance the idea of belonging to any particular 'party' within the church. His reaction to the efforts of such a party to secure a particular result in a church election resulted in a heated debate which lasted for two days in the Church Assembly. "Whilst in Melboume The Church Assembly sat and a warm discussion took place in which I bore a part upon an attempt by means of combination to secure the election of persons of particular sentiments as the 'Triers' in our Ecclesiastical Courts. This most unwise and unseemly indeed immoral proceeding was to my surprise condoned by the Assembly as the ill-doing had the countenance of the Dean & party calling themselves Evangelical who are the majority—but in reality the motion as put by me was carried & the more the subject has been since discussed the more has the improper attempt to pack a jury been condemned."

The *Church of England Messenger* described what happened in this way: "A debate of unusual warmth, extending over two whole days, and in which most of the leading members of the Assembly took part, arose upon the motion by the Rev. Dr. Russell of the resolution 'that in order to preserve the purity of the Spiritual Court of the Diocese, it is undesirable that any combination be entered into to control the election of the panel of triers for ecclesiastical offences.' The resolution, while affirming a principle which no one could deny, was so manifestly aimed at a private meeting of a few clergymen held some days before in the house of one of their number, that the Assembly refused to pass it, and adopted in its place an amendment by Sir W. F. Stawell, 'that the Assembly, thoroughly recognizing the undesirability of forming combinations with the view of controlling the election of the panel of triers or any other election to be made by the Assembly, deem it unnecessary upon the facts before them to express an opinion on the subject of this motion and do therefore proceed to the next order of the day.' Sixty-one clergymen and fifty-seven lay representatives voted for the amendment, to twelve and nineteen against it."

The *Messenger* commented in its editorial: "...by the judicious amendment of a layman the sting was taken out of the original resolution, and an opportunity given to the Assembly for affirming the principle without affording a triumph to any party within the Church. Thus the reverend mover, declining to act upon the advice of a friend and withdraw his motion, was deservedly left in a small minority, of whom several, we believe, very reluctantly voted with him. Such was the not discreditable issue of the first serious conflict which has occurred in our Assembly. The noise of the strife has now ceased, and we pray that God, who is 'the author of peace and lover of concord', will give grace to all who were engaged in it mutually to forgive any irritating language which they may have used toward one another."

There were other occasions when Francis Russell took part in the deliberations of the Church Assembly with the result of achieving the accord of those present. He also was nominated as a member of a number of select committees appointed by the Assembly. One of these was concerned with the lack of an adequate number of clergy to minister effectively in the Diocese. The Revd P. Homan moved that a select committee should be appointed "to enquire and report on the best mode of most speedily securing the clergymen now urgently required for the diocese... The Rev. Dr. Russell, seconded the motion, and suggested that the motion should run, 'That the Committee should inquire into the best mode of extending the ministrations of Divine worship in the colony.' (Hear, hear) The alteration being made, The Rev. Dr. Russell proceeded to say that there were large districts in which not a clergyman was to be seen, and even in Melbourne the ministrations of the clergy did not reach sufficiently home to the people, owing to the paucity of their numbers. He believed that, by an increase in the number of clergymen, the intellectual wants of different classes of minds would be better met. (Hear, hear.)

"The Church of England allowed a large latitude to its children. Some might prefer an almost histrionic form of worship, and others a very homely style, and the peculiarities of both, and all intermediate grades, were possible according to the spirit of the liturgy. There were several different forms of worship- the morning prayer or matins, the litany, the Communion, an extempore prayer, such as the bidding prayer and sermon (suited to Puritanical habits of mind especially). All these tastes and wants might be met, and clergymen, too, might be obtained, who would not shrink from illustrating their Sunday ministrations by the aid of science and ecclesiastical history, and so forth, as was now the habit to a large extent in London. The reverend gentleman concluded by alluding to other benefits which would flow from the appointment of such a committee, mentioning in particular the possible establishment of cathedral worship... The motion was carried unanimously."

Francis Russell enjoyed particularly good relations with Bishop Perry and Mrs Perry. "When Dr. Barker (metropolitan Bishop) visited Melbourne for the purpose of making arrangements whereby the Australian dioceses might through representatives confer together and agree upon uniform courses of action, Dr. Russell was, for several days by special invitation a guest at Bishopscourt. Bishop Barker and he then met for the first time, and the intensity with which the big Bishop looked long and curiously into the face of the man whose rare individuality he had often heard of, was most interesting to witness. A meeting was held which took the form of an entertainment to which Mrs Perry, assisted by several other ladies, invited the leading members of the Church; and, when a cordial vote of thanks, proposed by Bishop Barker, was unanimously accorded them in recognition of their kindness and hospitality, Dr. Russell, by particular request of Mrs Perry and other ladies, replied on their behalf in words of which they graciously signified their approval..."

Not only was there a personal basis to the agreement which existed between Bishop Perry and Francis Russell but there were also ecclesiastical matters on which they agreed. This was evident in the latter's acceptance in Melbourne after his dispute with Bishop Broughton. The matter was stated quite bluntly in The Argus at the time.

"EPISCOPAL— The Bishop of Melbourne has received under his episcopal superintendence, and has given employment in his diocese to the Rev. Messrs Russell and Beamish, the two clergymen of the Church of England, whose evangelical principles rendered them so obnoxious to the Puseyite Bishop of Sydney, that they were some months ago deprived of license to preach within his lordship's spiritual dominions. We hear that several others of the evangelical clergy of the Church of England in the Diocese of Sydney, find themselves so uncomfortable under Bishop Broughton that they contemplate resigning their charges in order that they may place themselves under the episcopal superintendence of the Bishop of Melbourne."

Bishop Perry's attitude was indicated in the first of three "Rules which the Bishop laid down for himself in his relation to the clergy of the Diocese." 1. Never to ordain, or admit into the diocese, a man, who, I had any reason to believe, held the doctrine of Christ's presence, in any sense whatever, in the bread and wine upon the Lord's Table after consecration; or who would encourage auricular confession with the object of receiving private absolution.

There was one matter on which Francis Russell was in complete agreement with his Bishop, and this was on the question of the desirability of parochial endowments. He believed "that strenuous efforts ought to be made in every parish to provide a small permanent endowment in order that the parish clergyman might not be wholly dependent on the free will offerings of people; and he held, with Bishop Barker, that in order to induce people to endow, a moiety of the patronage should, in each case, be offered in exchange for an endowment." When attending the sessions of the Church Assembly, "He seldom lost an opportunity of urging the great importance of providing parochial endowments, without which it seemed to him, that church progress was too insecure; and that which he urged upon others, he at his own cost was forward to promote." Francis Russell would be pleased to know that as a result of his influence many of the churches in the Wannon area have received endowments which still augment the stipends of the local clergy.

Closely related to the question of endowments was that of the payment for the services of the Church. Francis Russell was emphatic that "for no one of the Church services ought any charge, either direct or indirect, to be made." He "earnestly protested against mere voluntaryism, knowing that it often varied with men's wayward fancies and caprices; and he equally eschewed any arrangement that looked at all like selling Church ordinances." Later, after visiting the United States, he was to make this comment about the American Church: "The, so called, voluntary system places the ministers utterly at the mercy of the Vestry or Church Committee, and it is common to hear that Mrs So-and-so is offended and must have the pastor out."

"His views on these points were worthy of every respect, and his experience was most interesting; for his conduct accorded with his principles. Though he so loathed what is wont to be called the voluntary system, he was, perhaps, the only clergyman in the colony who so submitted himself to it as to have full experience of its practical working. For, rather than appear to charge for religious services, he not only never demanded but he never accepted a fee; he never suffered a sitting to be let in any of his churches, and he would not even allow a collection to be made in church for the benefit of the parish revenue." This was the reason behind the stress laid on the fact that there were to be no pew rents in the advertisement for the opening of Holy Trinity Church, Coleraine. Unfortunately, later this position was changed by those who did not have the same principles or faith. It was a position which was perfectly in harmony with the Rubrics of the Book of Common Prayer which when referring to the collection of alms of the congregation directs that they are to be used for the relief of the poor rather than in support of the parish. However, the Prayer Book did provide that every year at Easter each parishioner should pay to the Parson "all Ecclesiastical Duties, accustomably due, then and at that time to be paid."

A particular instance of Francis Russell's position was the question of marriage fees. According to the Prayer Book it was necessary to read the Banns of Marriage for the couple, usually on the three successive Sundays before the marriage took place. If it were desired to dispense with this requirement, perhaps because the couple wished the ceremony to take place in less than three weeks, then the clergyman could issue in the Bishop's name a licence to do so, for which it was customary to charge a fee, part of which was forwarded to the Bishop's Registry. Francis Russell refused to charge any marriage fees, and as we have already seen this fact was well known in the district. Peter Beamish commented on his friend's position in the appreciation which has already been quoted. "Those who objected to his not supporting the Registry by issuing marriage licenses, did not always remember that his refusing to take money for licenses was in accordance with a general principle to which he consistently adhered, and in carrying out which, so far as money matters went, the loss to the Registry was as nothing by comparison with the loss to himself. His parishioners did not trouble or consult him about ways or means where he was personally interested; they placed his stipend to his credit in the bank without even mentioning the matter to him. It was not always a liberal one, but at any rate ordinary men should be restrained by prudential considerations from copying in such matters one who was by nature so able and attractive as was Dr. Russell."

Francis Russell himself wrote a statement in 1873 of his position with regard to marriage fees which was "sent to a friend who at the time was in Melbourne attending a meeting of the Church Assembly." He begins with the question of fees: "I contend that no court holden can order money payments—that an imposition for the sacred offices of the Church is not allowed by our polity unless as a free offering, that the divergence from the constitutions arose by corruption as an ill custom and ought not to be perpetuated as though 'twere the very law of which 'tis a gross abuse and crying scandal." This is a reference to the rubric in the Prayer Book Service for the "Solemnization of Matrimony" which gives directions concerning the giving of the ring: "Then shall they again loose their hands; and the Man shall give unto the Woman a Ring, laying the same upon the book with the accustomed duty to the Priest and Clerk..."

In the first English Prayer Book the old custom of the Bridegroom offering his Bride "tokens of espousal" as well as the ring was retained, but these tokens of gold and silver were replaced in the 1552 Prayer Book by the payment to the Priest and Clerk. A nineteenth century treatise on Church Law commented: "It appears that anciently no fee was demandable for marriage, but only a voluntary offering was made, of what the party married thought fit to give. As in many other cases of the same nature, the voluntary offering became a customary payment, at first probably in particular parishes, afterwards more generally, so that a customary fee for marriage, varying in amount in different parishes, and supposed to be demandable as a customary right, has up to the present time prevailed very generally, and was long since recognized by the rubric in the office of matrimony." A decision of the Court of Queen's Bench at the time "recognized the validity of custom as regards a moderate fee for marriage, but ruled that thirteen shillings is an exorbitant sum."

Francis Russell next turns his attention to the claim that the issuing of licences to dispense with Banns was necessary when less than three weeks notice of marriage was given. Originally the relevant rubric at the Prayer Book service read: "First the Banns of all that are to be married together must be published in the Church three several Sundays or Holy-days, in the time of Divine Service, immediately before the Sentences for the Offertory; the Curate saying after the accustomed manner...." In 1753 in the reign of George II a law was passed which provided for the publication of Banns at Evensong when there was no morning service. Then in about 1809 the printers began to alter the rubric to conform to the supposed meaning of the statute. The rubric now directed that the Banns should "be published in the Church three several Sundays, during the time of Moming Service, or of Evening Service, (if there I be no Morning Service,) immediately after the second lesson".

He starts from the position that in Victoria the celebration of marriages is regulated by the Victorian Marriage Act of 1853. "The Act of George II stands repealed by our Victorian Act so that the present form of the rubric to be found in our Common Prayer-book should at least return to the condition in which it came from the houses of convocation, i.e. that is with the 'or holidays'. Those who put any stress upon the clergy having a distinct voice in the framing of our formularies should know that the later edition of the Rubric received from the Act George II has had no sanction ecclesiastical. The practical difference is that banns put up on 18th October, St. Luke's Day, and on Sunday 26th and on today SS. Simon and Jude would suffice, and when holy days for which special epistles and gospels are scant, other holidays inserted in the kalendar would 'tis held, be good for the purpose. Of course the Church contemplated the use of public worship beyond the Hebdominal function. But to my mind the Church isn't to be reduced to the narrowness of a sect. It is as near as may be the nation in the aspect of resistance against evil and needless severance from the public acts and laws of the realm is schism.

As then in England we use the Imperial Act as our rule in preventing illegal marriages, why should we in Victoria strive to disassociate our rule from the law which binds all and confessedly is framed the more effectually to bar wedlock not according to the will of Christ? Surely this is no fit place for raising revenue. 'Tis not a question of ways and means, but of fostering and promoting the sacredness of holy marriage and drawing more closely that mystic tie which if lax sets loose the worst evils that can afflict mankind. Banns have by the abuse of licenses been made the mark of poverty, and as they are not much of real guards, let us follow the better law we have (by the grace of our *lex loci*) at hand; at all events not make the banns cumbrous, by insisting under repealed George II on three weeks publication, and odious as going contrary to the present feeling in favour of decent privacy widely spread through society for the purpose of driving people to buy licenses at a heavy cost to a poor couple, new beginners in the expenses of housekeeping, and incurring suspicion for the Church that she cries up the sacredness and necessity of her wares to enhance the price to her customers.

If this be persisted in we must look for a growing disinclination for the blessing of our rite, and so work by our greed for the dishonour of holy marriage, and reducing the union of the sexes to mere bundling. I stand up for the rights of Church folk to solemn ordinances without money and without price; to the holy sacraments, to the apostolic rite of confirmation, to holy marriage, to Christian burial, and with my whole heart I exclaim against any attempt upon the part of bishops, priests, deacons or lay representatives to enforce payments for the performance of duties which, by vows made at ordination, the clergy have bound themselves to perform, and which are the heritage of Christ's people, poor as well as rich, to receive.

"These are opinions I have, as you know, long entertained, and with which I am I deeply penetrated. Preserve the foregoing, as there may be need to put my sentiments in print, and I can't find time on retiring to my parochial duties. I would be glad if the bishop would let you read them over, for we're not at one on the subject, and he, as bishop, asked me to yield up my will in this matter to him. *Nolo leges Anglicanæ ecclesiæ mutari."*

Chapter Fourteen

As we have already seen, Francis Russell was introduced to the processes of the Law and some of its practitioners at an early age when he lived with his uncle Sir William Cusack Smith. Sir William was but one member of a distinguished legal family. He was a Baron of the Exchequer in Ireland as had been his father before him. Previously, while Solicitor-General, there was one occasion when he and his father went to the North-East circuit together as Judges of Assize— a most remarkable occurrence. His father, Sir Michael Smith, *Bart.* was also the first Judicial Master of the Rolls in Ireland, and later his son, F. T. B. Cusack Smith was also to hold this same position. It is no wonder then that we are told that Francis Russell often met "judges and other leading men of the day" at his uncle's house. Similarly, when it came to deciding what his future career might be, there was strong pressure from some members of his family to take up the Law.

Although he finally decided that his vocation was to be found in the church, Francis Russell always retained a keen interest in the Law. Remember the interest he showed in studying Civil Law while speaking to the Revd T. B. Naylor and Mr Dowling on Saturday 2nd June 1849 and his hope that sometime he might proceed to a "degree in that science". It appears that he was able to find the time for the necessary reading and study amongst all his pastoral duties in the District of the Wannon. From about 1860 he is referred to as "Dr Russell" but there are still some questions to be answered about the nature of his doctorate. First of all there is some confusion as to whether the degree he held was D.C.L. or LL.D.. The former is to be found in the advertisement in the *Hamilton Spectator* in 1861 for the laying of the Foundation Stone of St John's, Digby and inscribed on the trowel presented to him in 1865 when he laid the Foundation Stone of Holy Trinity, Coleraine. The latter appears in Memoirs which were published in the *Church of England Messenger* and the *Ballarat Church Chronicle*. Second, it has not been possible to find any details of the conferring of either of these degrees upon Francis Russell. For example, there is no record at Trinity College, Dublin of his receiving an LL.D. from the University of Dublin and that institution does not have a D.C.L. degree. Similarly he did not receive any degree from the University of Melboume.

It may be that the title was assumed in anticipation of its being received formally at some later date. This was apparently the case with Peter Beamish . As early as 1861 he is referred to as Dr Beamish in the account of the opening of St John's, Digby in the *Hamilton Spectator*. But the History of Christ Church, Warmambool published in 1910 has this to say on the subject: "When visiting the old country in the year 1871, the Rev. P. T. Beamish attended the commencement of T.C.D., and received the degree of LL.D., which some years before, had been conditionally assigned to him, together with the degree of Doctor of Divinity, for which he had to preach before the University, twice in Latin and twice in English."

Francis Russell's interest and knowledge is to be seen in his letters to young friends who were starting out on their legal careers. Edmund Cooke was working in a Solicitor's office in London and a letter to him includes these comments: "I dare say you have full occupation and that you have at the end of the days work little spirit left in you to read Fearns Contingent remainders or Sugden on Powers. Alas! you see how entirely I am of the bye gone age for such text books are I guess out of date & form no part of the study of the new generation."

He then went on to make some observations about lawyers. "My experience of attorneys is that they seldom know the ground of the law they practice. Principles are lost sight of and either they council gross blunders or have at every fresh turn of a case to gain directions from one learned in the law. Surely there is no right reason for this and tho' in extensive practice it may be well to keep to one's tether yet in common affairs & with a moderate clientage an attorney should be well versed eno' in law to advise without losing skill to engross. In some of the colonies there is no distinction between the branches of lawyers, it is so also in the U. States & the tendency is to do away with any broad line of demarcation. However it is convenient even where no difference exists by law for advocates & counsellors & Equity draftsmen to keep to the branch they best know and have most repute for skill."

Reference has already been made to Francis Russell's letter to Sam Winter Cooke about the wording of the trust deed for the Parsonage land on the Wannon. His discussion of the points at issue betrays his interest and understanding. In a number of instances he quotes cases where the judgement given bears on the discussion. He concludes his letter with this query: "Have you seen Macaulays introduction to the Code for India? The novel feature of the Code is the plentiful exemplar cases like Titus and Bavius of the Codex only that these examples are made ruling illustrations under the statutes."

By contrast there was at least one occasion when Francis Russell found himself the object of the attention of the due process of the law, as the following report shows. It is taken from the *Hamilton Spectator*, Wednesday 12 April 1865.

COLERAINE POLICE COURT

On Monday last, at Coleraine, some cases were heard under the Scab Act, before Messrs. Fetherstonhaugh, Turnbull, and Trangmar. The Rev. Dr. Russell was fined 1s and costs for having unbranded sheep in his paddock; Mr Robertson of Struan, one shilling and costs, for the non-registration of brand; and Mr R. Learmonth, of Tahara, £30, for a sheep infested with disease belonging to Tahara run being found on the Struan Station. It was stated, after a thorough examination, no disease had been found among the sheep at Tahara, and that consequently, the sheep must have become infected after leaving that station. Under the Act, the Bench had no alternative but to inflict the penalty. There were a few debt cases of no public importance.

Francis Russell also earned a rebuke from the State Registrar General for having been slow in conforming to the provisions of the Registration Act of 1853 which provided for the compulsory registration of births, deaths and marriages with the Registrar General's Office. Before this time church registers contained the only records of Victoria's Vital Statistics, and these were not really suitable for statistical purposes. The new Act came into force in 1854, but no marriage returns were sent from the District of the Wannon until the beginning of 1856. This omission came to light when a request was received for details of a marriage which Francis Russell had solemnized in 1855, and resulted in the following correspondence:

Bishop's Registry
Melbourne

July 20 1871
My Dear D Russell

I send you on the other side copy of a letter received by me from the Registrar General on the subject of Tackley's marriage— I presume that he considers a statement by me of the obligation you are under to transmit copies of registration of marriages solemnized by you to his office will have more "influence" with you than one made by him. It is undoubtedly the fact that Clergymen under the Law which came into operation in the year 1855 are bound on solemnizing marriage to register the same in the form thereby prescribed and to transmit quarterly to the Registrar General a copy of the registrations so made by him during the currency of the quarter. The failure to comply with the law in these respects subjects the clergyman in default to a penalty in respect of every default of a sum of not less than ten nor more than fifty pounds.

I remain my dear D Russell
Yours very faithfully
Tho T a'Beckett

The Rev D Russell
Parsonage
on the Wannon

(copy)

Registrar General's Office
Melbourne 19 July 1871
Sir
Referring to your letter of the 13th *inst* in which you state that the Rev'd Dr. Russell has sent a certified copy of Tackley's marriage to England, I beg to point out that no entry of the marriage in question is recorded in this office, and I should feel obliged if you would use your influence in obtaining from Dr. Russell a duplicate of the same, together with any others which he may have celebrated in the year 1855, for record and reference as by law required.

I have &c
(sd) W. H. Archer

The Registrar
of the Diocese

Bishop's Registry
Melboume Augt 3 1871

My dear D Russell
Mr Archer referred to the return in his office, of marriages solemnized by you and ascertained that the first return from you was made in January 1856. The act came into operation in April 1853.

I am my dear D Russell
Yours faithfully
Tho T a'Beckett

The Rev D Russell

The Chief Justice has the appointment of Guardians of Minors and he is now absent on leave in consequence of ill health—I expect to see Dr Redmond Barry tomorrow and will shew him your note and ascertain whether he as Senior Judge in the absence of the Chief can make the appointment.

The marriage records were eventually straightened out by Francis Russell's assistant at Digby, Mr R. J. Mercer. He also wrote up the Baptismal Register in the most elegant handwriting and as he mentions in the following note he bundled the various roughly written original records according to the year. These still remain a fascinating collection in the Parish of Holy Trinity, Coleraine.

Digby, Octob. 16th 1871

My Dear Dr. Russell,
I enclose herein a memo of some particulars re the marriage registers; you will find each year's papers made up in separate packets, & you will have no difficulty in finding the dates referred too [sic], as they follow in order.

In returning these Books & Papers, I have to express regret on two accounts—first, that you did not give them to me earlier, that so I might have had more time to spend upon the writing, and could have compared the

Baptism memos with the original documents, and so have obtained some "maiden surnames" still wanting— I do not however despair of doing this in the future— my second regret is, that the work is done, —I can truly say, that nothing I ever did, has given me such pleasure, and parting with the books, seems like saying good bye to old friend — the completion of the work, seemed to leave a blank in my existence. You will find the Baptisms indexed; there is also a separate index to the Marriages, which may facilitate reference.

I am, my dear Dr. Russell
your faithful servt
Rigbye J. Mercer
over

October 21st
Since writing the within I have had an opportunity of comparing the book of Baptism Registers, with the original memos at the Parsonage & have found 3 errors & 3 omissions. I am also dissatisfied with my work in other ways, and therefore I am taking the book with me—its presence will enable me to converse with you in spirit at least.

Chapter Fifteen

"The question is often and eagerly asked what, (humanly speaking), was the secret source of the strange and subtle power for good which Dr. Russell unmistakeably had over those whose pastor he was? and it seems to some who were his bosom friends that they can answer this question.

"Bishop Perry, who ever admired and loved him, has been heard to say that 'in natural power none of us is his equal.' Mrs Perry's account of his social qualities was that he was always and easily 'king of his company. Physically, as a young man, he was capable of a vast amount of exertion and endurance, for after having been most of the day in the saddle, riding hither and thither, visiting the people in his immense district, he would sit far into the night over his books. But what most of all drew and knit the people to him was his inexhaustible sympathy. He could scarcely get close to any one without entering into sympathy with him, and without drawing him into sympathy with himself. Several simple gentle ladies who knew him only as a minister of consolation to them in times of trouble and perplexity, thus expressed their thoughts and feelings concerning him, 'There never was any one in this country like him, and there never will be.' And those who knew him best were convinced that he was different not only in degree but in kind from most other men. The Almighty had put upon him the stamp of genius, and in nothing had He more distinguished him than in the faculty wherewith He had endowed him of gaining men's confidence; of constraining them to confide in him as in one who, they knew, could counsel and comfort, soothe and solace, feel with and for them, whatever might be their sorrows or their sins."

This was the way Peter Beamish remembered his old friend some years after his death in a memoir published in 1891 in *The Ballarat Church Chronicle*. He was also affectionately remembered by Cuthbert Fetherstonhaugh who had been something of a 'bright spark' at the time. First of all we have his memories of some of the people who lived in the district and then we have the description of a lively incident which brought him into personal contact with Francis Russell.

Samuel Pratt Winter

From a photograph, ca 1870: Manuscripts Collection, State Library of Victoria, MS10840

"Winter was a most delightful man to meet, intellectual, kind, and generous. He, like Acheson Ffrench, very early adopted the Darwinian teaching, and consequently both were looked upon with great suspicion by the orthodox; indeed, as already stated, Ffrench was designated an atheist, because he professed belief in what the majority of educated clergymen now teach from their pulpits. Good Parson Russell, whose parsonage was not far from Murndal [the home of Samuel Pratt Winter], and built on land presented by Sam Winter, must have had many a discussion with the latter on this and other interesting subjects. They were fast friends. Dr. Russell was not only clever and intellectual, but one of the best men I ever knew."

"When I had settled to go to Queensland I went to Tahara to say good-bye to Bob Learmonth, and at night, when I started for home (it was moonlight), we decided we would have a lep or two by way of farewell. I was on Pannikin, and Bob was on old Tommy Racquet, both good fencers. we got over the horse paddock all right, and then into Dr. Russell's cultivation paddock, when down came Tommy Racquet over a heap of stones, and Bob lay on the ground stunned, with his face cut and all over blood. It would not do to let Parson Russell know about our pranks, so I jumped Pannikin back out of the paddock and hung him up a bit away, and went back to Bob, who by this time had come to, but was quite dazed. To mend matters, I saw a man coming towards us from the house. I bundled Bob on his horse, and gave the animal a cut of my whip, sent him out over the fence, and Bob disappeared. When I went for my horse he was gone, and I had to walk back to Tahara.. There I found Bob in bed with his face badly cut, but the groom had washed and dressed it. I had to get back to Muntham that night to get some fat cattle for a Portland butcher, so took the stable horse.

"When I got near the Parsonage I made up my mind to call in and make a clean breast of it to the parson, as he was such a really fine fellow, but before reaching the house I met a man on Pannikin. I said, 'Where are you going?' He replied, 'For the police. This is Mr Fetherston's horse, and we think he has been stuck up.' I said, 'How do you know it's Mr Fetherston's horse?' 'Oh.' he replied, 'We opened the valise and found his name on a collar.' (Moral: Never have your linen marked if you are up to larks.) I said, 'I am Mr F.; is Dr. Russell at home?' He said, 'Just come home, and he is in a great way; Mrs Russell and her sister thought the place was going to be stuck up, and they got a terrible fright, and Mrs Russell is quite ill.' This was very pleasant for me. However, I rode on and met Dr. Russell and tried to explain matters to him; he was, however, very angry, and after making all the apologies I could I rode off. I returned next day, and made my peace with the ladies over a cup of tea and was forgiven, but poor Bob's face was so bad for some time that he could not call, and it was a long time before he squared up matters at the Parsonage.

"Dr. Russell was a splendid man, and beloved by all who knew him. He was a model 'bush parson,' and welcomed by high and low. I never remember any bush clergyman who was more universally beloved and respected. He was highly educated and clever, never pulled a long face, or depicted religion as something sombre and lugubrious, but he was a deeply religious man, and one in whom there was no guile."

Examples of his care for the people of the district may be discovered in his letters. First an extract from a description of a visit to Melbourne in 1870. "My other motive for the visit to Melbourne was a sad letter we had about Miss Chambers she was teazed with the desire to see me no doubt a sick fancy but the tidings of her state were so grievous that I was unwilling to deny her wish. Poor girl! She knew me I spoke of death to her which her family had refrained from doing and 'twas evident to us all that tho her mind had sunk into imbecility yet that serious feelings could be awoke & that underneath there was love to God & resignation to His most mysterious dispensation."

In a letter to a young man who was seriously ill he again raised the question of the importance of being prepared for death. "When one's bodily strength is much wasted and the natural spirits agitated and deprest it is only too common for friends to avoid conversation on serious subjects and to go on awaiting for a more favourable condition which may not come at all or when present is not used as was intended and thus I fear is brought to pass what happened in the case of George the IV when his last seizure came 'What is this? Oh! they have deceived me, it is death!' were his expiring words. Surely however kindly meant it is better that we should know all beforehand & make that timely preparation for the great change that soon, or late comes to us all. Sickness seems sent that our thoughts should be detacht from the things temporal and lifted up to the Eternal and dark & drear as the vision is when it crosses the imagination when the world looks bright & our human affections and hopes firmly grasp at the illusions of earth. I know from many an instance that this is not so for long when the languor of disease sets a gloom upon the spirits & forces us to see that this world consists of unsatisfying joys, many trials and sorrows and sore disappointments to all who have minds to think and hearts to feel. How blessed then if we can only make our own the rest which remains for God's people it giveth to the heart songs of rejoicing in the loneliness and darkness of our night-seasons. This is indeed the peace spoken of in the Gospels the power of Christ resting upon us which sets us above infirmities, and all the sad & changeful conditions of our earthly life— the love of God shed-abroad in our hearts by the Holy-Ghost (like oil poured over the troubled waters making a 'great calm') that love which when made perfect casteth out all fears."

By way of illustration Francis Russell then went on to tell of his experience in counselling one of his parishioners, and this story is one of the most moving episodes in all of his letters. "Whilst you were at home in the end of '66 I had the aweful duty of breaking to Mrs Murray the sad intelligence that her days on earth were numbered She had been lately married to a husband who was devoted to her not only was she a lovely young woman but she exercised over him & others a rare fascination under which softness & sweetness she had strong sense & sound principles All the circumstances of her position promised a full fruition of her fondest longings for happiness. They were wealthy and for the first time she had the power of doing all that her heart desired & her mind inclined to— On her wedding-trip she caught a severe cold rapidly symptoms of tubercle on the lungs developed and the Physicians despaired of her recovery.

"All that took place on the day she learned the true nature of her state is imprinted on my memory ˜ Dunrobin (their place on the Glenelg) was beautiful under the clear sunshine the garden in which the poor girl took much pride was gay with flowers She met me with her usual grace & cheerful welcome and for sometime was busied in displaying the valuable presents her father in law had sent her for he (a sour stern old man) was doatingly fond of his son and his new daughter. I could not find it in my heart to say what I had come to tell at last I askt her to kneel with me before God and then in words addrest to God her father I said all. She arose startled trembling all over adjured me to keep nothing back & whilst as tenderly as I could she heard the truth her hands were clasped upon her knees keeping down emotion She exclaimed my husband! my parents! & must I soon leave all! I spoke of the glorious hopes— and of the Divine gift of peace and bade her rely upon the tenderness of her Saviour & that strength would be given according to her needs— she wisht to be left quite alone and afterwards we could perceive how pious resignation grew into earnest hope and when at last death came she declared that she had fulness of joy— she wrote some affectionate words in her diary which she closed for ever with feeble hands put her wedding ring on he husband's finger and with a face radiant as tho' already she possessed the beatific vision entered upon her rest.

"The secret of her joy was that she believed in God as her father reconciled unto us, sinners by nature and by our own misdoings, by the mysterious incarnation of the Only begotten Son; Whom He in His love and pity to us spared not but gave up for us all. She found rest for her heart's burden on the close sympathies & exceeding greatness of the love of her Redeemer & in her innermost spirit she had the witness of the Holy Ghost attesting to her oneness with Christ in His sufferings and in His resurrection by her unfeigned mourning for the transgressions of her youth & her estrangement from her God and the genuine horror she now felt at sin as sin and her conscious liberation from the thraldom of evil and that her heart rose up in longings for the manifestation of the sons of God & complete deliverance from the bondage of corruption into the glorious liberty of the children of God."

Francis Russell then went on to speak of the way in which we should live our lives in response to the love of God. Finally he included some practical advice. "Many have told me that they have found it most useful to have particular times for devotion

1. to reflect before engaging in prayer to use helps to keep before their minds, sins & wants & causes for thanksgiving

2. to examine their own consciences closely every day taking the commandments and Beatitudes at beginning of V S. Matthew as a standard-rule

3. often to receive the Sacrament of Holy Communion

4. Every day to read with much pondering a portion of the Gospels and a Psalm; & if sleepless by night to repeat collects, hymns & verses of Scripture learnt by heart

5. To read also a set part of the Old Testament every morn and of the New Testament other than the Gospels every even.

6. To read or have read aloud pious books

Beveridges Private thoughts
Pascal Pensees
Taylors Holy living & dying

but tastes vary so much that one mind can hardly pick out in the (thanks be to God) wide range of devotional literature what is most suitable for others.

"All controversy should be put away as poison & such trifling conversations or light amusing reading as our own experience tells us unfits our minds & hearts for the great work on which we are set thro' the help of the Holy Ghost to accomplish that we may have that true knowledge of God which is eternal life and gives abiding Peace.

"God bless you and receive these lines as a mark of the wishfulness of my heart that whether it be the will of God that your days on earth be many or few when the destined hour strikes you may find that for you to die is gain.

"Many some you know not make prayers daily before God for you

ever affectionately yours

F. T. Cusack Russell"

Chapter Sixteen

Francis Russell wrote letters of advice to those in health as well as those in need. Two years before he wrote to Edmund Cooke about the need to prepare for death he had given him advice about Christian living. "Your mother's heart is bound up with your welfare & if ever Temptation stands by your side egging you on to do what conscience bids you not to do let the thought of your Parents broken in spirit by your wrong doing incline you to give heed to the voice of conscience urging you to the good & true.

"My reading & reflexions & observations have taught me that religion is the only sure stay in times of great trial and that religion in the soul of man is a delicate plant in an unkindly soil and that if from one cause or another we omit habits of devotion our reliance upon God— His guidance His protection His mercy is torn up by the roots. Liveliness of feeling in matters of religion is good but as nought when compared with 'patient continuance in well doing'. I wonder whether Sam attends the lectures of the Master of the Temple given to Members of the Inns of Court on the New Testament.

"In London it is not easy to get acquainted with the clergy of a Church but the best way is to call upon the particular clergyman one wd wish to know & signify your desire & take part in some work for the benefit of others & the furtherance of Christ's Kingdom . . . For all that is wild & repulsive & harmful in religion has its origin in the effort to divorce faith in the Lord from the practice of His precepts. So I trust my dear boy even in the vast whirlpool of London you will do something tho' it be little to manifest your sense of God's love to you by actively helping on to a happier & better life those whose daily walk is by your side."

In 1872 he wrote a letter to 14 year old J. C. Hassall, who had just gone to Geelong Grammar School, in which he included good advice mixed with news from home.

"My Dear Jimbo,

I very much regretted not to have seen you to say farewell before you left, but you have been in my thoughts, and may God bless and keep you in His own care. Be truthful, never sly, never try to darn cobwebs, or screen your faults. Keep the rules of the school and of the house loyally. Don't, dear boy, be cowed or dispirited should you be behind hand with your tasks— the fling you have had will naturally make application dull and hard at first, but persevere. 'Dogged does it.' The power of keeping your thoughts on the subject before you, of remembering what you learn and of combining what has been acquired before with the stock in hand— all this comes easier and easier with every fresh struggle.

"When I went to Wootong Vale the place seemed to Mrs Russell, Miss Smithson, and myself, empty without you. Your Mamma told me how George had pined at your loss, and as she said this she took long breaths, went off to the fireplace and began to poke the logs that had no coals— but we knew why this was— and if you want to give her comfort and joy be a good, brave, true-hearted, and diligent boy.

"------- puts himself to be your particular friend, and I should like to hear of your being partners in everything.

"Louisa and her man stayed a day with us, and we were charmed to see that she was happy and improved in manner and looks, without losing one point of her old frankness and gaiety of heart. Could you have seen your Juno-like sister, as from the chariot— yclept by us 'buggy'— she graciously inclined her noble head and waved her adieus you would have been struck with amaze.

"Write when you have time and inclination, and say to me whatever you please.

Believe me, dear Jim,

To be ever your affectionately

F. T. Cusack Russell"

Similarly he wrote about the Christian life in a note to James William Trangmar.

"My dear young friend

I thank you for your letter and very kind appreciation of the slight help I was able to give you. Nothing occurs just now to my mind to add only this be diligent in studying the Bible strive earnestly to do your Heavenly Father's Will as it becomes revealed to you this will cost effort & self-sacrifice but remember that keeping His Commandments is the channel the Blessed Jesus points out as the mode of testifying our love towards Him and this combined with the promise of a most sweet mystical and ineffable indwelling of the Godhead with us and be this infixt in your soul that there is but one thing strong and sure on Earth and that is the power of prayer.

"May you be blessed in body in mind and in spirit is the prayer

of your affectionate friend

F. T. Cusack Russell

"We are always anxious to hear good news of your Uncle and that your Aunt is by God's grace keeping up hopefully and bravely

Give her my kindest regards

"Parsonage on Wannon

13th August 1873"

By contrast, when Francis Russell wrote to Sam Winter Cooke, who had begun work in Melbourne, he had some advice for him about his physical and social well-being rather than spiritual.

Parsonage on Wannon

by Coleraine

March 13th 1872

My Dear Sam

I have often promised myself the pleasure of writing a few lines; but this & that came betwixt the wish & the accomplishment. O course we keep ourselves well informed of all your doings and can follow you from S. Kilda [to] Mr Well's Chambers & look in upon you drafting and settling bills in Equity and plaints at law for I hear the practice is a general one and embraces both jurisdictions of the Supreme Court and adjourning to the Club for lunch— this part of your daily life your mother and I settled in *petite comité* for we agreed that the walk at mid day on the shady side of Collins Street would help on appetite & be a diversion & that at the club you would have good food according to Dr. Johnson's formula 'well fed, well killed, well-kept, well-cookt, well served.' Which I doubt cannot truly be said of the Melbourne eating-houses not even of Scotts or Menzies. Besides it is well to rub up against the *creme* of our Victorian Society & learn by a sort of insensible contact the feelings & prevailing modes of thought which find an embodiment there in squatters, merchants, journalists, Doctors, lawyers, and gentlemen at large.

"The *creme* I fear me is poor stuff not worth the skimming but it is well to understand the people amongst whom our life is cast & I remember that Bright when but a star of the lesser magnitude was accused by the Editor of the *Times* in an angry altercation of roaming up & down the live long day clubs & Parliament-House gathering up flying rumours & battening upon bits of gossip— *Voila* the result!— Your walk homewards and morning 'header' we can fancy too and heartily do I wish that I could join myself to you in your strolls. Life in Melbourne is too bustling; too little contemplative for my liking. The men you converse with push their fancies & thoughts off upon you as if nought of all can be gain-said or if they allow argument it is a sharp *recontre* all for Victory whereas I think it is most pleasant to discuss & unfold subject one mind getting one aspect another another view & so enlarging the field of intellectual vision & moral sympathies."

Francis Russell's distaste for town life was one of the reasons why he remained for so long in a country parish, but there was another reason which was brought out in Peter Beamish's Memoir.

"The question has probably suggested itself to some, why was a man of Dr. Russell's exceptional powers allowed to labour for a quarter of a century in a sparsely peopled district? Does it not seem as if he were specially qualified to be a leader in one of the great centres of population? A sufficient answer to such enquiries is that, once he became attached to the people at the Wannon, nothing would induce him to leave them; he was of a very affectionate nature, and he clung to his friends, even when he was well aware that his bodily and mental health as well as his financial position would have benefited by a change. Thus on the 7th October, 1859, he wrote to a friend, 'I have a constant pain along the course of the Ischiadic nerve, and am beginning to be conscious of a distaste to horseback, but yet I would be no denizen of a town.'

"Later he wrote, 'I received an invitation to take Sale,' (Tempting conditions were proposed, as superior income, house, &c., &c.,) 'but,' he adds, 'I stick to the Wannon; I suppose this poor frame will be Wannon dust yet.'

"Again in 1861, 'I have had a letter from Judge --------, reminding me that the Church at Toorak, will be soon ready for Divine Service, and asking me to make up my mind.'

"In 1870 he wrote, 'I have had an offer of St. Paul's, Sandhurst, with a large, handsome church, parsonage, and income. As my income here has dropped low, and threatens to diminish owing to the critical state of many of the old stock, I am for the moment wishful to take a larger and surer berth; but old associations and the averseness to move swayed me and I declined.'

"In 1871, he wrote, 'The Bishop wishes me to take St. Paul's, Geelong, But I am disinclined to make a move, although I see clearly that greater difficulties will be felt than ever before to raise my stipend to a becoming support owing to the old families being embarrassed by the times.'"

In a letter to another friend in 1870 he also commented on the invitation to go to Sandhurst (present day Bendigo), which was now a flourishing gold-mining area..

"I have been much urged to leave the Wannon for Sandhurst which owing to the discovery of some new reefs & the well working of the alluvial deposits has sprung up into great prosperity & has shot ahead of Ballarat. There is a fine new Church &c. &c. but I am constant to my old love & altho' I am warned that my years are growing into a heavy burden so that shortly I must walk with tottering steps & that infirmities are coming on apace yet I care not to gain more ease of body & have a chance of 'laying up' for this seems the 'refrain' abandon old friends & places & betake myself to a new sphere amid new acquaintances. The Bp wishes me to take S Pauls Church Geelong & in some respects this wd be more desirable than Sandhurst."

However, he was not tempted away from the familiar friends and places which meant so much to him.

Chapter Seventeen

The Colony of Victoria was given responsible self-government in 1855 and the first parliament, consisting of the Legislative Council (Upper House) and Legislative Assembly, met in 1856. One of the first Acts passed provided for universal manhood suffrage for elections to the Assembly but since there was no payment of members until 1871 not everyone was in a financial position to stand as a candidate. In the Upper House members had to fulfil certain property qualifications and electors to that house also had to have either property, educational or professional qualifications. It wasn't until 1908 that women were given the vote on the same terms as men and as late as 1950 before the restrictions were removed from the qualifications of members and electors of the Legislative Council. Although the privileges of land-owners were very important in this system of government by comparison with other groups in the community, one important feature which would be significant in the development of more democratic structures was the use of the secret ballot in elections from 1856 onwards. (It was used then for the first time in any British community.)

In the Western District it was to be expected that the pastoralists would play a significant part in politics since they were more likely to be able to give the time than could other men in the community. Many of them also believed that they had a responsibility to make a contribution to their local community and to the colony as a whole. They contributed generously to building funds for local churches, encouraged the development of educational and cultural institutions with their time and money and offered themselves as members of parliament.

Francis Russell accepted the prominent position of the pastoralists in the life of the times. In 1861 he commented in a letter to Samuel Pratt Winter: "I see Fairbairn is back again and old Mackersey by degrees we are getting all the old Australians and a happier day would dawn up in the country if gentlemen of position would take their proper in public affairs— Indeed there are very few cases of the rejection of a gentleman of good standing by any constituency and if the legislature has fallen into low hands the fault perhaps is with gentlemen standing aloof from politics."

George Fairbairn had been associated with Fulham and Congbool stations and then became a successful gold-buyer in Ballarat after trying his luck in the gold rush at Bendigo. In 1854 he married the daughter of George Armytage of Fulham and took his bride to England. They had just returned in 1861 and during the next thirty years he would prove to be a highly innovative and hard-working pastoralist with extensive interests in Victoria and N.S.W.. Fairbairn was elected to the Legislative Assembly in November 1864 but he was a silent member and did not enjoy politics. He withdrew in January 1866.

If Fairbairn was a reluctant politician there were others who were more than ready to serve in the legislature. John Alexander MacPherson had lived in the Western District and managed Croxton, one of his father's sheep stations. In 1858 he married Louisa, the daughter of Cuthbert Fetherstonhaugh, the police magistrate at Hamilton and thus was the brother-in-law of young Cuthbert who got into strife jumping the fences at the Parsonage one night. He nominated as a candidate for Dundas, the electorate around Hamilton, in 1861 but then withdrew in favour of another candidate, W. Mollison. He did enter parliament in 1864 as member for Portland but was member for Dundas from 1866 to 1878. He was a minister in several administrations and was premier himself in 1869-70.

Henry John Wrixon had attended school in Portland and then studied Law at Melbourne University and Trinity College, Dublin. He returned to Victoria in 1863 and as we shall see attempted to enter parliament in 1864. This attempt was unsuccessful but in 1868 he won the seat of Belfast (Port Fairy) as a radical reformer of the land laws and the Legislative Council. He had a long career in politics as a member first of the Assembly then of the Legislative Council, where he was admired for his sincerity and eloquence. He was a mixture of radical and conservative. He supported the Hare system of proportional representation, female suffrage, the Saturday half-holiday and worker's compensation for injury; but he did not agree with the payment of members of parliament and had a fear of socialism. He was knighted in 1892. Here is a letter from Francis Russell to Samuel Pratt Winter, written in response to Henry Wrixon's attempt to gain support for the election in 1864. Notice his comments about the relationship between Church and State.

8th July 1864

Parsonage on Wannon

Dear Mr Winter,

We had all made up our minds to go to Murndal yesterday when the rain set in as we fancied for the whole afternoon I hope to see you soon. Mr Wrixon wrote to me pretty much in the same strain as his letter to you I do'nt know how it would be possible to assure him of an unopposed return but with your interest and Quigleys assistance with the aid of good distinct principles and all set off with a handsome elocution I think he might reckon on distancing all competitors. Of course some candidate will come forward on the principle of giving everything to everybody & so ignorant and gullible are a large portion of the electors that he may rely on a following but I should expect Wrixon to be ready enough to shew-up the absurdity of his opponents. To give good farms at low rates & seed corn & ample meats & rations for the first year would sound sweetly in the ears of the masses as also would protection of native indolence in the shape of bounties to home cobblers & wheelwrights & hatters & tailors & farmers but Wrixon is I suppose well up in Political economy and able to point out the fallacies of protection.

The danger is that as a political adventurer he will trim his sails to catch the popular gale if so he will go down in a lurch. What the country is feeling after is a man of independent mind and fixed views— moderate conservatism— who sees not only the rocks of despotism but the shoals of democracy. Wrixon must come up & hold forth & begin at the beginning endeavour to indoctrinate the constituency into the elements of political knowledge and I think he must make out a good case for some Material advantage to the district such as the Railway to Hamilton this would give cohesion to his supporters & enlist in his favour the rich and poor the capitalists & workers of society throughout the district.

Macpherson relies on brass & too openly comes forward as an adventurer. Darbyshire is the worst foe for he I am told is extreme & wishes for occupation licences. Watts I should be sorry to see as representative of these counties he is an ill-tempered fellow with a biting gibing tongue & like all men who have lived long in Melbourne is all for centralization even tho' he may speak to the contrary. I was sorry to see in Wrixon's letters anything about the religious interest he has nothing to do with churches as a Politician only to see that the system adopted be fairly carried out.

I would most strongly dissuade him from relying upon the Church of England as a party that it is not & there in does it differ from Romanism & from the Protestant sects. Education should be made accessible to all without any hindrance. I think the Shire councils should be remedied. assimilating them as nearly as possible to the English system (placing certain members ex officio on the Board)

There are some law reforms much needed e.g. succession to real & personal property simplified & made less expensive where the reality is under £---- value. The circuit court should also be held at Hamilton The County Court at Digby or Casterton. Matters of this sort are really important & could gain votes where large measures would be uncared for.

Mr Fairbairn is not anxious to get into the assembly. He is not a speaker & if he would give his interest & support to Wrixon would be valuable. Then there is Swan & Turnbull & Geo Robertson. If you could write or see these folk it could much advance Wrixon but care must be taken to avoid anything like secret canvass. A meeting at Coleraine & Casterton & Redruth & Hamilton might easily be arranged & feelings tested & then a --------- signed requisition could be forwarded to Wrixon a meeting at these places would'nt involve much speaking.

I do not like doing anything in the way of a direct canvass— 'twould not become me to do so. But if you and Turnbull & Mackersey Carmichael Tackett and others made an arrangement to attend the several meetings & put forward Wrixon he might calculate on success if in his personal canvass he comes up to the mark.

I return the speech as he sent me one.

With kind regards from Mrs Russell & Miss Smithson

Believe me

yours sincerely

F. T. Cusack Russell

In a letter to Arbella Winter Cooke in 1870 Francis Russell commented on recent political moves involving the extension of the state's transport system and of the further separation of church and state. "There is more prospect of Railway than ever. McCullock has pledged a certain expenditure on such public works & that soon the Western District shall be opened up. The Portland line which is a necessity for the farmers will be got on with.

"The State grant in aid is to be withdrawn after five years I shall lose about £50 a year & the loss will fall most heavily on our Churches (structures) but I suppose with the new ideas of political society this was inevitable— The Assembly mean to transfer the amount saved from religion towards payment of members. The proposed grant of £7000 to Grant who thro' drunkenness has made himself incapable of holding office is a sad job. And surely a blemish on the Colonial state of society that could make such a proposal possible."

James Macpherson Grant had been a member of parliament since 1855 and had made some important contributions to the State, especially through his two Land Acts. In April 1870 he was dropped from the ministry, probably because of his ill health resulting from his fondness for drink. He persuaded the government to withdraw the £7000 because it threatened a constitutional crisis. He re-entered the Assembly in 1871, in better health, and his financial worries alleviated by a public subscription of £3000 and the introduction of the payment of members.

The letter to Mrs Cooke ended in a reflective mood. "I am writing as if you were in the chair opposite & pt when you read what I have written or even whilst I write. What awful changes may be present to turn my thoughts if all things were known into a different current. Now & then the clear perception of the future— the eternal opens up before me & I am over-whelmed. I have some letters written by an uncle from India 1807 full of boyish enthusiasm he had just joined his Regiment & was giving to his father an account of the new friends & scenes he had found & asking many questions about home and whenever I read these letters I vividly realize the time when I & all my contemporaries shall be things of the past & yet not of the past for we shall be still in being but how & where?— The true view of human life is to recollect that God is a Father & that here we are preparing— i.e. in training, acquiring the habits which we are to take with us into the Eternal world. God helping our weakness & pardoning our many offences. I humbly trust we shall meet again if not in this world yet there where there is fulness of rest & peace & joy. Tell Cecil I have my debt on my mind. With our most affectionate greeting to your brother & sons

believe me

ever most sincerely yours

F. T. Cusack Russell"

Chapter Eighteen

Francis Russell's active service in the district of the Wannon was brought to an end in 1874. At the beginning of the year "he was returning from a long trip in his parish, and was driving a pair of quiet ponies in his buggy, when he was seized with a paralytic stroke. He was alone, and was as yet some miles from his parsonage. There was at least one pair of gates to open. Fortunately, the stroke was not severe enough entirely to disable him, for he succeeded in accomplishing the task, though it involved getting out of his trap, and climbing back into it again after opening, and leading the ponies through, and closing the gate again." (E. S. Jackson Notes p31)

"He managed to reach his home where he was taken care of at once. Dr Charles Smith, of Casterton was sent for. For some weeks the patient, by his orders, was kept very quiet." During this time he was visited by John Jackson from Sandford, to whom he remarked that he must soon be getting back to work. Mr Jackson reminded him that the Doctor had recommended that he take extended leave and perhaps even visit the old country. "The patient pointed out that to him that was impossible owing to the paucity of funds, for, said he, 'You know what I am.'" This remark prompted Mr Jackson to begin a collection to help Francis Russell to undertake the necessary leave so that he might regain his health. He was assisted in this by Samuel Pratt Winter of Murndal who wrote to him on 20 February 1874.

"My dear Mr Jackson,

I received your note of the 18th inst. last evening and agree with you that no time should be lost in giving the amount collected to Dr. Russell; any sum subsequently contributed can be placed to his credit. I don't think a break-fast or any public notice (as if we were paying him a compliment) would be desirable— it is merely our act of duty and justice to place a sum to his credit with Bank to enable him to recover health, imperilled in our service with utter disregard of his own temporal welfare. . ."

He then went on to list those who had given or promised contributions and set out a draft for the letter which might be sent to Francis Russell: "With the deepest concern your parishioners & friends have heard from the Bishop that Dr Macrea considers your arduous and incessant devotion for such a long period to the duties of this large district has seriously imperilled your health and that complete rest is absolutely necessary for its restoration. Your parishioners and friends earnestly entreat that no feeling of responsibility will enduce you to slight this advice— and altho' your absence will be deeply felt they fervently hope it is God's will that your health shall soon be restored and that you may long live to influence and cheer the lives of your devoted friends & parishioners.

"To aid in defraying your expenses during your absence I have been requested to place to your credit in the Bk of ----- the contributions at present in my hands..." As a result of these efforts we find the following letter written by Francis Russell to Samuel Winter.

"12 George St.

Melbourne E.

My Dear Mr Winter,

I cannot trust myself to write more than a few words, but I think would burst were to repress my feelings so entirely as not to say how deeply I am grateful to you for the new instance I have just received of a friendship which has never faltered ever since you first knew me. Yesterday I received an announcement which quite overcame me that a thousand pounds have been put to my credit at the Bank with the expression of kindest feelings on the part of the contributors that it be used for the rest the Physicians so strongly recommend me. If I knew myself at all it is not the largeness of the gift but it is the generous warmth of affection shown by it that touches my feelings & leaves me scarce power to say 'God bless you'..."

He then goes on to speak of travelling to England through America in order to cut down the long sea voyage involved in the other route and also to visit places of interest in that country. Mrs Russell also had a sister living near San Francisco whom she had not seen for twenty-eight years.

By June they had reached America, but the journey had not been as easy as anticipated. "The voyage had been so disagreeable Mrs R. was emaciated and quite feeble, so that a month's rest was requisite to restore her." He mentions that while in San Francisco he has taken the opportunity to find out as much as possible and sets out a variety of impressions. "The amazing fertility of the soil surprises me and the prowess shown to till the soil with the least employ't of manual labour. The rapid extension and cheap maintenance of Railways so that the produce is rapidly and cheaply brought to ports of embarkation. As regards govern't we have in the example and practise of this state much to learn in order to avoid. The judicial executive departments are foul indeed. Elephantis and leprosy, small pox and malignant fevers are prevalent in San Francisco and stringent measures should be taken to avoid their introduction to our Colonies. A great part of the labour is done by Chinese on farms as well as household work. Of society, so far as comes under my observation, there is little sociability but much display. The great object of the rich is to have a fine house sumptuously furnished, and then run off to Europe to expend on the grandest hotels thousands of dollars. Books are not read as in Melbourne and the eternal talk is of shares, all are bulls and bears in turns [with] great sums lost & made daily."

He was also impressed by the surrounding countryside with the variety of its scenery including forest with many different flowering shrubs and also the geysers. However, he was most impressed by the farming. "We went southward to St. Clara & San José and were charmed by the richness of the soil and extent of cultivation and absence of any sign of poverty. What compels one to wonder is the size of the cultivated farms and the houses— substantial edifices with 100 acres of fruit trees— Everything on a grand scale."

In New York the Russells missed meeting the Revd W. Kennedy Brodribb on his way to minister to the people in the parish of the Wannon. While there Francis Russell visited a number of other towns including Boston, Cambridge, Philadelphia, Baltimore and Washington. "Philadelphia interested me most from its order, cleanliness & the comfort in which the working classes evidently lived." In New York Mrs Russell and her sister met their brother and his family. "They had not met since his boyhood & it was a pleasant reunion. He has the management of a factory & large business & resides at a pretty country house on Staten-island."

Francis Russell also has a comment on the elegant homes of New York. "The marvellous uniformity of the finer houses on 5th Avenue & the off-lying streets surprised me. All seemed as built after one unvarying model & a slight thing read me a lecture on the social condition of a community forced in every way to economize labour. In the finest furnisht house I ever saw with all the sumptuous console tables, ormolu & pier glasses in every room, the personal washings were supplied by lavatories common to each story & a handsomely carved box in each proved on opening an apparatus for blacking shoes!" This was instead of a servant bringing water to each individual bedroom and there being someone to clean shoes when they were left at the doors at night, I suppose.

In matters ecclesiastical Francis Russell commented that the English Church was prospering. "...the clergy have large salaries & certainly imprest me as splendid elocutionists."

They sailed to Ireland in the "*City of Paris*" and had a good crossing. They stayed there with relatives of Peter Beamish. He had this comment to make of the country, in a letter dated 28 September 1874. "I find Ireland here wonderfully improved, farm labourers get house, not the old mud cabin but a substantial stone & slate cottage, fuel, the loan of a cow, a plot of potatoe ground and from 9/- to 12/- per week, with additions at harvest. Stewards, which you remember mean in this country working-overseers, get £50 a year & large allowances. The potatoe for the first time since the famine years is both good and abundant, but the desire for Emmigration is so rife that small farmers are ready to part with their holdings & go abroad & so the farms are fast becoming consolidated & in the hands of a Protestant Yeomanry."

"Certainly all the Churches about here, & they are very numerous, are well constructed with nice Rectories & good glebes, but ultra puritanical in the avoidance of all ornament even to a cross on the gable & quite a row occurred here at the introduction of brass eagle lectern presented to the Church of Queenstown. Your beautiful windows at Coleraine [the five in the western wall given by S. P. Winter] wouldn't escape injury from these fierce iconoclasts as we saw from the wanton injury done to painted lights in the Church of Timoleague gn. by Col. Travers as a memorial of his daughter."

There is an appended note which gives a report on his health at this time. "...and tell Dr Macrea that I hope to write to him soon, meanwhile I obey faithfully his injunctions. The strange sensation has much gone from my hand & I think myself greatly improved in health & energy; my obesity is much diminisht." In another letter to S. P. Winter, dated 21 January 1875 he again touches on this subject. "I had a sharp attack of inflammation in left lung & was obliged to cross the channel. In England at Clifton & afterwards at Malvern I grew quite well & strong & I'm flattered by my wife who dreads that I am growing too young for her. I have lost flesh & my face is less like a full moon."

Sam Winter had written asking him to sit for a portrait to be painted by Stephen Pearce. Francis Russell writes, "By the bye yr sister gave me yr. message about the pictures, & of course I willingly comply with yr. kind request." In later letters we are given progress reports on the painting. (7 April 1875) "I am to sit & you wd. have inly laught as I did at Pearce's glance at me. What kind of portrait-worthiness there was in me sorely puzzled him -------- a boon companion, a successful raiser of pigs, or --------- of a noted 'crack' for Melbourne Cup. So he awaits tomorrow my first sitting to ascertain how I am to appear— as 'guide philosopher & friend' or 'with eye in fine phrenzy rolling'." (5 May 1875) "I have given some sittings to Mr Pearce; as yet I haven't lookt at his work, this pleases him better & he thinks he'll make a true picture. For the life of me I can't frame a serious visage, when he looks so long & scrutenizingly at me, so that I shall descend to posterity as *'Jean qui rit'* instead of the more rueful & reverend Father. One thing indeed distresses me, that you should think it worth while to spend so much upon such an unworthy object." (no date) "The portrait I haven't seen, but Mr Pearce seems to go on prosperously & has invited Mrs Bomford to a view this week. Said he to me the other day, I wish to make it a 'Speaking' likeness for your *forte* I take to be as a 'conversationalist' & Mr Winter wd wish this to be rendered. I was greatly amused, for somehow he conceives I must be somehow a 'celebrity' & thus he solves the enigma." (August 1875) "I had my last sitting yesterday. Pearce seems to have caught an excellent likeness."

There are actually two paintings, one at Murndal, the other hanging in the Dining Hall at Trinity College in the University of Melbourne.

Francis Russell's Portrait

"From the original Life-sized Portrait painted by Stephen Pearce for Sam[l] Pratt Winter Esq." and engraved by Alex. Scott.

Chapter Nineteen

At the beginning of 1875 Francis Russell felt well enough to undertake some light parish duties. "Just now we are in Leicestershire. My brother wants to go away on business & finds it impossible to get a curate & has strongly urged on me to take his duties for 3 Sundays. The Bp. told me (Bishop Perry had returned to England in 1874) I was wrong to yield, but as I look full of vigour it wd cause a breach betwixt us were I to refuse. The Parish is quite a country one Hugglescote. The former Dean of Cashell McDonnell is now at Leicester, Vicar of S. Mary's & we are school fellows & very attached in our boyhood & he has asked us cordially to see him there." (21 January 1875)

In a letter of 5th May there is a hint of other work to come. "Thro' the Bishop I have been promised a temporary Chaplaincy during the summer months. This will suit my pocket for somehow the cost of travelling & staying in London is such as at times to make me feel uncomfortable." Later he writes of other prospects. "Yesterday I was offer'd a chaplaincy at the opposite end of L. Geneva from G. The Hotel des Avants with half my own Hotel charges & £2-2-0 weekly, the duties very light, & afterwards in the Grisons at the Baths of Bormio. Of course travel is very costly & as I judge it right to save all needless expense I'm glad of this offer & especially because we mean that Herbert shall pass his summer holiday with us as our guest."

Francis Russell was able to take up his appointment and gave the following account of their travels in Switzerland and Italy. "...we had been in Switzerland which we enjoyed much— I had become a good walker & Mrs Russell travel'd a' foot thro' the valley of Chamonix. Sleep, appetite good, the little 'services' on Sunday in no wise fatiguing. We then travel'd further into Italy & we made the journey a great exertion by endeavour to see all that was interesting. For instance at Milan we arose at 4 o'cl spent some hours in the Duomo, then we passed from the bottom to top of L. Como, then spent all night in Diligence with very bad fare (my part was chiefly unripe pears) & late in the afternoon got to Bormio."

Unfortunately Francis Russell was not to continue to enjoy this good health. The course of events is outlined in two letters written on 7 July 1875, the first written by himself to Sam Winter and the second written by Mrs Russell to Mrs Cooke.

Bormio. Italy

7th July 1875

My dear friend you will excuse a short note from me as I fear just at present to write at further length. We since you last heard have been spending some weeks at Montreux & here at Baths very celebrated under the Roman Empire & now resuscitated with a great Hotel in the midst of scenery— the Sellvio ascent on one side & the Engadine on the other, with in front the long gradual ascent from Lake Como the Vittelline way— very grand and lovely.

Yesterday I felt particularly well & had just despatcht a letter to Bishop of Melbourne saying how well I was & that Mrs R. enjoyed this place much & telling him I wished to return to my home & work & accept Josey's invitation for Christmas Day.

In the afternoon my wife, a young lady staying at the Hotel, & myself went for a walk. We strolled about charmed with the effects of the landscape, when I felt numbness in my right thumb which I fancied might be from pressure of a cane I carried, then a stiffness & cold sensation in my right brow and cheek (to which I called my companions attention) & then the power of articulate speech failed me.

This was a recurrence of the old attack of Feb 1874 from which I had been completely free ever since. I found that neither distinct speech nor the power of understanding words of a book which I tried to read remained with me.

After a night's sleep I feel now, just as yesterday, quite well, but I must be prepared for all God may send upon me.

Your kind heart will be grieved & my own strong hopes of perfect recovery blighted.

If I be able I shall write soon again and with earnest prayers for your long continued health & happiness & of Josie & Will's & Trevor's not forgetting Miss le Camp.

Mrs R. will write to Mrs Cooke.

I am your grateful & attacht friend unto death.

F. T. Cusack Russell

Will you kindly tell Miss McLeod when you see her I had intended writing to her but cannot do so now.

Bagni

Bormio

Italy July 7th

My Dear Mrs Cooke,

I had intended writing you a long letter telling you how thoroughly we entered into your joy in the birth of Josie's little daughter but I am in too great distress to do so now but I would not like you to hear of Frank's illness from any one but myself. Ever since our visit to ------- his listless irritable-ness had almost disappeared as well as the irascibility of temper he used to be troubled with and seemed quite happy even without books. The day he was taken ill he was feeling and looking remarkably well & asked me if he did not look so for that he felt his skin so soft and was sure the air here was particularly healthful and spoke of going out to Australia to eat his Christmas dinner with you all. In the evening as we were walking he felt the twitching in his face & thumb & when he tried to address a lady who was with us he could not do so distinctly. Next day he felt better & wrote to Mr Winter but soon afterwards the pain came on again in his head and he could not make himself understood & has been in a kind of sleep or light headed ever since. We are quite isolated here, there is not a lady in the house (as from some unaccountable cause the Baths have not been much frequented this season) nor can any of the female's servants speak English. I feel it is a judgement for I was always haunted with the thought of going out to the Colony without my sister.

Now dear Mrs Cooke I hope you will excuse my writing so much about ourselves but I know you take an interest in all that befalls us. I had written to Herbert telling him he was to join us here but I know not what plans will be now.

. . . And now dear Mrs Cooke with much love to yourself Mr Cooke & Cecil. Believe me your affectionate friend.

Margarette Russell

The course of Francis Russell's illness is outlined in letters written after his recovery to Sam Winter and Dr Macrea. After recounting the attack which affected him while walking in the evening of the 6th July he continues: “The next morning I found speech, but I knew that an attack was approaching fast, which being the third I supposed was likely to be fatal. I did not wish to affright Mrs Russell, I went to Breakfast & walkt about (having wrote a few lines to Mr Winter & the Bishop of Melbourne). I had an intensely painful headache & then became quite unable to speak & the arms & hands beyond my control. I never thought of an Italian Physician & ‘twas late on Thursday when the Dr, who turned out to be surgeon of German Education & skilful, came to see me. He was almost despairing, but he had me removed to the Baths (natural sulphur & warm), this brought down the pulse from 120 to 90, he then used cathartics &c. He thought from the first it was apoplectic but provoked by indigestible accumulations in the bowels. Day after day I lay, not quite unconscious but unable to recall the simplest words such as bread or to attach any idea to Lord’s prayer when repeated. Every day castor oil was administered & very gradually my intellect grew clearer, voluntary power returned to my hands, & speech more slowly came back.

“Still if I grow weary my power of recalling words is difficult. Mrs Russell tells me that I have been unconscious, and I fainted off, when she supposed I was in the act of dying. It disturbed me a good deal to think that she was quite helpless & friendless out in the Grisons in the event of my death & my unknowing of what she should do. I do conjoin the treatment with recovery...”

“...the sinking of the vigour was beyond what I could have supposed in so short an illness, for the day of my attack I had felt well & was blaming myself for eating the bread of idleness. Poor Margarette became ill from care & watchfulness night & day of me. She was a little cheered when the Doctor told her he had hopes of my life when he had brought down the heart’s action. The air was quite cold in Bormio & there was ice close at hand which was kept constantly to my head & all the people were most kind & attentive. The Bishop got friends to write to Hotel Proprietor & wrote with much sympathy himself. It was very strange as I grew convalescent, I had much effort in recalling after many trials word by word the Lord's

Prayer, connecting meaning with words; & the reading was by letters as a child & I had to ask what i. t. & t. h. e. spelt."

"I fear to look into the future, not believe me about money matters but I dread dumbness or idotry... I fear the seizure of my intellects & Mrs R. tells me of the pitiful looks & groans when I couldn't express the thoughts I had or wishes... I never feel God's love more than while awaiting the last step from time into eternity. God's mercy to me a sinner. There is an interweaving of God with us; a life, a light proceeding from God into us & a peace resulting. Sin shall not have dominion over us for we are not under law but grace. These are the mysteries revealed at such moments, and I think there is coming to me the true meaning of your distaste of dogmas. The truths are living powers or they are a mockery, a delusion, a snare; & the insufficient efforts to put these felt truths into adequate words raise up among us evil spirits of bigotry, falseness & intolerance."

"Dr Smith (from Casterton) has just past the afternoon with us. He says if I return soon to the Wannon it must be on the assumption of taking little, if any, duty. This distresses me, to interfere as I must if I take upon me the incumbency without putting all the force I have in the duties. Yet I have a strong wish to go home, my home soon. Indeed the only counter-vailing force is the weak state of Mrs Smithson which detains her daughter [Lucy] with her, who has been so great comfort to my wife."

After his recovery, the Russells travelled through Switzerland to Zurich and then by train through the Black Forest and on a boat along the Rhine as far as Cologne. Their immediate destination was Holland and the home of a family, one of whose sons lived for a time at Murndal.

"By the Loisel family we were most hospitably entertained. we should have gone to Maestricht, in fact were on our way, when a lady addrest me at a station en route, asking whether I was *M. le Pasteur*, & who urgently begged us to descend from the train. This was the daughter who with her brother had visited all the day long train after train to intercept us.

"We came on a long house, chateau-like & found an apartment ready for our reception. Apartment a suite of four rooms, very elegant. The father quite a gentleman of *'ancien regime'*, the mother of a Dutch family (originally from Protestant French refugees) very kind & motherly & the daughter somewhat like Mr Kerr, girlish in appearance so that we were astonished to find in her the mother of two sweet children. The son at home is Burgomaster & a scholar, proud (& justly so) of Leyden where he has been educated. The other son was at our visit absent with his regiment— Dragoons. M. Loisel was for many years in India & spoke English fluently, the daughter quite as a native & the mother always read English books, but couldn't use it conversationally."

Chapter Twenty

By August 1875 the Russells had returned to England, but Francis was still determined to return to Australia. On 9th November 1875 he made his will.

"Being now sound in mind & mindful of the uncertainty of life I make this as my last will. To my dear wife Margarette I bequeath all I have fully for her own uses & maintenance & hereby constitute her my sole executrix knowing that kind friends will assist her by wise counsels.

F. T. Cusack Russell

"Signed by me in the presence of us who sign in presence of testator & each other on the 9th November 187five

Susan Murphy Flora Murphy

"Should we die before the voyage to Australia be completed I appoint Rev'd Dr Beamish, J. H. Gregory, S. Pratt Winter Esq & J. H. Jackson as my exors & trustees with full powers to expend any or all money I leave for the benefit of the Church of England in the Ecclesiastical District of Wannon-cum-Glenelg, diocese of Ballarat where I have laboured. By we aforewritten I mean my wife & self. I further ask the Trustees in latter case to consider Lucy Smithson if she need, to have the yearly interests of £1000 applied to her during her life.

"Signed by same persons as before under same circumstances.

F. T. Cusack Russell

Susan Murphy Flora Murph"

On the 5th January 1876 the Russells sailed from Plymouth in the sailing ship "Hampshire". Miss Lucy Smithson apparently remained with her mother who was in ill health and needed someone to care for her. Francis Russell had sought the advice of Sir Wm. Gull about the voyage home and he had recommended that he make the voyage by a sailing ship and avoid the excitement of a royal mail steamer.

“Although warned by his medical adviser, before leaving England, that it would be unwise to attempt anything like work for some time to come, he had regularly conducted divine service twice each Sunday, from the time of his joining the ship at Plymouth. Few of us are likely to forget the simple earnestness with which, at the close of his first service on board, after alluding to his physician's warning, he told us that he could not let the sacred day pass by, without assembling those who were willing, to join with him in Christian worship.

“It may be that these Sunday labours hastened the end, but we feel sure that he himself would have chosen, had the choice been put before him, to die as he had lived— in harness.”

(The Hampshire Weekly News)

They had proceeded a month on their voyage and had passed the equator when on Sunday 6th February “after he had twice on that day conducted service on board, and had spent some time among the sailors instructing and advising them, he complained of headache, and he was obliged to go below and seek his berth. As he laid himself down, he said, ‘I will say my prayers in bed to-night.’ These were the last words he was heard to utter.”

(P. T. B. Memorial Sermon)

“...although evidently unwell, his indisposition was attributed to the intense heat that prevailed, and it was hoped that a change to cooler latitudes would remove the unfavourable symptoms. About three o’clock on the following morning, however, he was seized with a sudden and alarming illness, and, although every possible aid was rendered, both by the skilled medical officer of the ship and by one of the saloon passengers, a physician who had made this class of disease his special study, Dr. Russell never recovered consciousness, and at five o'clock in the afternoon he breathed his last.”

(The Hampshire Weekly News)

HEALTH REPORT

For the week ending 9th February

Cases treated to termination	8
Under treatment	2
Death	1

Total	11

For the week ending February 16th

Cases treated to termination	5
Under treatment	3

Total	8

Remarks

The death reported during the week ending 16th inst [sic] is that of the late Reverend Dr. Russell. The Reverend gentleman was attacked at 3 o'clock on the morning of the 7th inst. with severe and rapidly recurring epileptiform convulsions, having no less than eleven fits in four hours. These were followed by compression of the brain, coma, and death at 4.15 pm on the same day. I have not the slightest doubt that the primary disease was atheromatous [curdy] degeneration of the cerebral blood vessels.

During the second week the majority of the cases treated were accidents, arising from falls, &c.

R. DENHAM PINNOCK, M.B.

Surgeon

(The Hampshire Weekly News)

"The burial of the late Rev. Dr. Russell took place on the afternoon of Tuesday, the 8th inst. At five o'clock the slow and measured tolling of the ship's bell warned all who wished to pay the last tribute of respect to our late friend and fellow traveller to be in readiness. Shortly afterwards the crew were mustered in front of the lee gangway, which was open. The passengers now congregated on the break of the poop and on the main deck,— at a quarter past five. All hands uncovered as four sailors, bearing between them something covered with the Union Jack, emerged from the cuddy door, went slowly forward to the gangway, opposite to which they deposited their burden, and then stood aside. All knew what that burden was, and few were present who had not at some time during the voyage received kind looks and pleasant words from the now closed eyes and lips. And now, from the same door, comes our captain, followed by the doctor and chief officer, and take up their position a few steps from the body. The first-named, in an impressive voice, reads the burial service (the doctor acting as clerk), and at the words 'commit his body to the deep,' the flag is lifted, a splash is heard, and the quiet ocean receives into her bosom the earthly remains of one of whom it may be truly said that he died at his post."

(The Hampshire Weekly News)

Index

www.ingramcontent.com/pod-product-compliance
Ingram Content Group UK Ltd.
Pitfield, Milton Keynes, MK11 3LW, UK
UKHW020128250726
13967UKWH00002B/531

9 781445 771731